# Warrior

In the years leading up to the war, America tried to maintain its neutrality. Even as her enemies became more aggressive, America managed to avoid being drawn into war

**Pearl Harbor, Hawaii**

7 December 1941
The Empire of Japan issued America
A brutal surprise invitation
to enter World War II.

All followers of Jesus Christ
are engaged in Spiritual warfare.

For Christians, neutrality is not an option.
We can wait for the attack, or
we can prepare for the battle.

Warrior
Revised 2019

Mike Wheeler
Birmingham, Alabama

Cover artwork provided by
Mrs. Jenny Thornton, Birmingham, Alabama

Warrior

# Contents

**The Mission**.................................................4
- A Call to Arms (1) ................................. 5
- Truman (2) .........................................19
- Heads of State (3) ...............................28

**Axis Powers** ............................................37
- The Big Lie (4) ....................................38
- Tojo (5) ...............................................49
- Schutzstaffel (6) .................................63
- Peace for our Time (7)........................76
- Aryan Paragraph (8)...........................88
- Fifth Column (9).................................101
- Operation Himmler (10) .................... 116

**Allied Powers** ........................................129
- Persecution (11) ................................ 130
- Suicide in April (12) .......................... 149
- Operation Overlord (13).................... 164

**Arsenal** .................................................178
- Joseph Goebbels (14) ....................... 179
- Dimples 82 (15) ................................. 194
- Gibraltar (16)..................................... 213
- U.S.S. Hornet (17).............................. 229
- P51 Mustang (18)............................... 243

Warrior

The Mission

# Purpose

## Objective

Warrior is intended to be a Bible Study to be used in a small group setting and/or as a personal study guide to take us deeper into God's Holy and infallible Word.

If you are using Warrior as a personal study, we encourage you to take one chapter each week and work through the study one section at a time. The most profitable way to study Scripture is to read it in depth, in context, and to dwell or meditate on it.

If you are using this study as part of a small discipleship group or home Bible study, we encourage you to work the study at home and come each week prepared to share your own insights with others in the group.

## Structure

Each chapter in Warrior is broken down into three parts. The first part is simply a story from World War II. The second part(s) are designed as reading assignments with opportunities to look at various Scripture verses that we have associated with the topic. The third part, entitled "Special Orders", is a summary of the chapter.

## World War II

This study is not intended to be an in-depth study of World War II and should not be taken as such.

We have taken anecdotal stories from World War II and used them as metaphors to illustrate principles related to the Spiritual battle experienced by all Believers. Many of the stories are taken from books and personal accounts of events in the war. Accordingly, these stories are colored by the opinions and viewpoints of the writers themselves.

## Scriptures

**John 15:4** says "Abide in me, and I in you. As the branch cannot bear fruit by itself, unless it abides in the vine, neither can you, unless you abide in me". The objective of this study is to draw us closer to Christ - and that will result from abiding in His Word and opening up our hearts to the Holy Spirit.

**Scripture Studies** – We have included Scripture references throughout this study. It is to your advantage to study these passages and, even more so, to expand your reading to other areas of Scripture.

**Other cited works** – We have included comments from other sources. While these writers do not carry the weight of Scripture, we believe them to be trustworthy.

## Scripture References

Unless otherwise noted, all Scripture quotations are from The Holy Bible, English Standard Version® (ESV®), copyright © 2001 by Crossway, a publishing ministry of Good News Publishers.

# Spiritual Warfare

"No soldier gets entangled in civilian pursuits, since his aim is to please the one who enlisted him."
**2 Timothy 2:4**

As followers of Jesus Christ, we are called to be disciples and we are called to make disciples of others. As disciples, we are engaged in battle against a formidable (yet defeated) enemy. Christ secured the victory on Calvary – but the enemy continues to fight and there are casualties and consequences of the ongoing battles.

Scripture tells us that our primary opposition is from Satan himself:

> "For we do not wrestle against flesh and blood, but against the rulers, against the authorities, against the cosmic powers over this present darkness, against the spiritual forces of evil in the heavenly places."
> **Ephesians 6:12**

But Satan is not our only enemy. Satan and his demonic host have influenced a world culture that is insatiable in its attack on followers of Christ, and we wrestle with the desires of the flesh that are regularly enticed by the world and Satan.

## Concerning Satan

> "There are two equal and opposite errors into which our race can fall about the devils. One is to disbelieve in their existence. The other is to believe and to feel an excessive and unhealthy interest in them"
> **C.S. Lewis** [1]

---

[1] Lewis, C.S. – *The Screwtape Letters*, C.S. Lewis Pte. Ltd. 1942

## Concerning the Flesh

"Now the works of the flesh are evident: sexual immorality, impurity, sensuality, idolatry, sorcery, enmity, strife, jealousy, fits of anger, rivalries, dissensions, divisions, envy, drunkenness, orgies, and things like these. I warn you, as I warned you before, that those who do such things will not inherit the kingdom of God."

**Galatians 5:19-21**

## Concerning the World

"You adulterous people! Do you not know that friendship with the world is enmity with God? Therefore, whoever wishes to be a friend of the world makes himself an enemy of God."

**James 4:4**

## Three Enemies in Concert

"The world is no friend to grace; our own flesh strives against the spirit; but ultimately, there is no man-hating enemy of the soul like Satan. Although he has no immediate power over the mind and soul of the believer, the devil knows how to use the world and how to play upon our fleshly propensities. He is the exquisite tempter; he knows how to snare souls and cause Christians to doubt the mercy of God."

**Thomas Brooks**

A Call to Arms (1)

## **Disciplines of Grace**

We will talk about disciplines of grace, accountability, Bible study, prayer, and other tools to strengthen our walk with Christ. However, we don't want to make the mistake of trying to earn God's favor by our works. God will not love you more based on the number of "quiet times" you have each week or the number of verses you have memorized.

**We have been justified by grace alone and we are called to live out the Christian life in the same manner.**

The world, the flesh and Satan are powerful spiritual enemies. But God is more powerful. His victory was secured when he put his own Son on Calvary's Cross. It was then and there that the world, the flesh, and the devil were defeated.

Even with the victory in hand, we are still called to the battlefield. And no warrior should ever go into battle without preparing – physically, mentally, spiritually, and emotionally. The spiritual warrior is called to carry appropriate weapons into battle. He is equipped with a sound battle strategy. He understands and believes in the mission. His leaders are reliable and battle-tested. His enemies have been scouted and studied for strengths and areas of vulnerability.

As Warrior disciples, we are engaged in a great battle and the stakes are high. Our Leader is perfect and his plan is flawless. Our call is to engage the battle.

# The Mission

In World War II, the Allies' mission was to stop the aggressions of the Axis powers in Europe and in the Pacific.

In the process, the mission was to free other nations that were victimized by the enemy.

For the Believer,
our Mission is to Glorify God and follow his command to live as image bearers of Christ and to bring His message to a world that is held in bondage to a powerful enemy.

# A Call to Arms (1)

"I am a pacifist. You, my fellow citizens of twenty-one American Republics, are pacifists too.

"But I believe that by overwhelming majorities in all the Americas you and I, in the long run if it be necessary, will act together to protect and defend by every means at our command our science, our culture, our American freedom and our civilization."
**Franklin Delano Roosevelt (10 May, 1940) - [2]**

Indeed, President Roosevelt did everything possible to avoid being drawn into the war that had engulfed Europe over the past two years. America was still feeling the pain and economic hardship resulting from World War I and the Great Depression.

## 16 March 1935
German Chancellor Adolf Hitler makes the announcement that Germany would no longer honor the Treaty of Versailles that ended World War I. His announcement was the first in a series of events that would lead to World War II.

## 31 August 1935
United States President Franklin Roosevelt signs the Neutrality Act, or Senate Joint Resolution No. 173, which he calls an expression of the desire to avoid any action which might involve the U.S. in war.

---

[2] 10 May, 1940 Roosevelt's Radio Address to the Eighth Pan American Scientific Conference.

# The Mission

The act included provisions restricting Americans from sailing on ships from "hostile" nations and imposed an embargo on the sale of arms to "belligerent" nations.

**15 September 1935**
In Nazi Germany, German Jews are stripped of many of their rights by Nuremberg race laws.

**9 May 1936**
Italian dictator Benito Mussolini invades Ethiopia.

**1938**
- March - Hitler announces the "annexation" of Austria
- August – Hitler mobilizes the German Military
- September – Munich Agreement is negotiated with British Prime Minister Neville Chamberlain
- October – Germany occupies Sudetenland, the portion of Czechoslovakia inhabited by more than 3 million Germans.
- November - Kristallnacht (The Night of Broken Glass), when Nazi's carried out a massive, coordinated attack on Jews throughout the German Reich.

**1939**
- March – Nazi occupation of Czechoslovakia
- May - Nazis sign 'Pact of Steel' with Italy.
- August – Germany signs 'non-aggression" treaty with the Soviet Union
- September 1 – Nazis invade Poland
- September 3 - Britain, France, Australia and New Zealand declare war on Germany.

**1940**
1940 saw the German invasion of Denmark and Norway (April), followed by the invasion in May of France, Belgium, Luxembourg and the Netherlands.

## A Call to Arms (1)

1940 was the year that Winston Churchill became Prime Minister of Great Britain and the year that saw a summer-long assault by German Luftwaffe on the British (Battle of Britain) – including air raids on the city of London.

Through all of these events, the United States held to its commitment to stay out of the war.

Instead, the United States provided other forms of assistance to Britain and other allies in Europe, including the "Destroyers for Bases" agreement signed by President Roosevelt in September, 1940. Under the terms of the agreement, the United States gave the British more than 50 obsolete destroyers in exchange for 99-year leases to territory in Newfoundland and the Caribbean, which would be used as U.S. air and naval bases.

Shortly thereafter, the U.S. entered into the "Lend-Lease" act (17 December 1940), providing even more support for Britain in the form of materials and supplies.

### April, 1941
America's first military incident involved an encounter between the USS Niblick and a German U-boat off the coast of Iceland in April, 1941.

### 4 September 1941
A German submarine fired on the U.S. Destroyer Greer. Two days later, the S.S. Sessa was torpedoed and the merchant ship the Steel Seafarer was sunk by German aircraft in the Red Sea.

### 17 October 1941
USS Kearney was torpedoed by a German U-boat in the north Atlantic, followed two weeks later by the sinking of the USS Reuben James.

Following the sinking of the Kearney, President Roosevelt did not ask Congress for a declaration of war on Germany. Instead, he chose to warn both Hitler and Mussolini that the United States would defend itself against their attacks.

| The Mission

**Pacific Theatre**
The lead up to World War II in the Pacific can be traced back to 1931 and hostilities between Japan and China, when Japan invaded northeastern China, establishing the Japanese state of Manchukuo.

**December 1937**
"Rape of Nanking" Although the actual death toll has been hotly debated, the Japanese Army marched into China's capital city of Nanking, killing 40,000 to 300,000 soldiers and civilians over a six-week period.

**1941**
The United States had suspended strategic trade with Japan, limiting their access to much needed resources to support their efforts to control the Pacific. In response, they turned their attention to Indochina and the East Indies.

The plan would require neutralization of the American Navy's capacity for retaliation.

**7 December 1941**
Pearl Harbor – Hawaii

The Empire of Japan launched a brutal surprise attack on the island of Hawaii in the early morning hours of 7 December 1941, inflicting heavy casualties in and around the American naval base at Pearl Harbor.

The day after the Japanese attack (8 December 1941) on Pearl Harbor, Congress declared war on the Empire of Japan. Three days later, 11 December 1941, Germany and Italy declared war on the United States.

Along with Pearl Harbor, the Japanese carried out coordinated attacks throughout the month of December 1941 that included:

Midway, Wake Island, Guam
Siam, Burma, Philippines, and Hong Kong

# A Call to Arms (1)

**America at War**

Following Pearl Harbor, American men and women enlisted to serve. Some served in the Pacific, some in Europe, and some in northern Africa. Some served as Admirals and Generals, others served as pilots and infantry, while still others served in mess halls or dug latrines. Some served the war effort at home, developing weapons or other support for the warriors in the field.

No matter the role or the theatre of battle – the mission was the same for all. The mission of the Allied forces in World War II was to stop the military aggression of the Axis forces and liberate the countries that had fallen to that aggression. The primary enemies in World War II were Nazi Germany (Adolph Hitler), Italy (Benito Mussolini) and Japan (Emperor Hirohito).

## Quest for Neutrality

America did everything she could to avoid being drawn into a war that had begun several years earlier with Nazi aggression in Europe and Japanese conquests in the Pacific. Pearl Harbor was the seminal event that drew us into the War.

For every follower of Christ, neutrality is not an option. Spiritual warfare was instigated by Lucifer's rebellion and his first victory was in the Garden of Eden. From that point on, Satan has been prosecuting a war on everyone who dares to follow Christ.

## The Mission (1.1)

*"The chief end of man is to glorify God and
enjoy him forever"*
**Westminster Confession of Faith**

Jesus came to earth on a mission. Nowhere is this more evident than in His conversation with Peter in Matthew 16. In verses 13-20, Jesus called Peter "The Rock" and told him "on this rock I will build my church, and the gates of hell shall not prevail against it."

But when Jesus told Peter he must go to Jerusalem, suffer, and die, "Peter rebuked him". Jesus' painful words to Peter were: "Get behind me Satan! You are a hindrance (stumbling block) to me". The "rock" was now referred to as "Satan".

Jesus' mission is revealed in the last part of verse 23:

> "For you are not setting your mind on the things of God, but on the things of man."
> **Matthew 16:23**

**John 6:37-40:**
From this passage, what would you say was Jesus' primary mission on earth?

_____

_____

_____

_____

_____

# A Call to Arms (1)

### Luke 4:16-20:
Jesus quotes a passage from Isaiah 61. Comment on the nature of Jesus' statement and its relevance to his mission.

_____

_____

### Matthew 5:17-18
What does the passage reveal about Jesus' mission in light of human history?

_____

_____

### John 17:6-8:
What does this passage reveal about the relationship between God (the Father) and Jesus (Son)?

_____

_____

### 1 John 3:8
According to this passage, what was Jesus' earthly mission?

_____

_____

_____

Jesus Christ came on a mission. That mission could only be accomplished by His suffering at the hands of the "elders, chief priests, and scribes", His death, and His resurrection.

Jesus came on a mission and was not about to be distracted by wealth, power, prestige, earthly kingdoms, and other things that the world had to offer. Jesus came to do the will of his Father. His mission was eternity.

| The Mission

## **Spiritual War (1.2)**

"The Lord God said to the serpent,
"Because you have done this, cursed are you above all livestock and above all beasts of the field; on your belly you shall go, and dust you shall eat all the days of your life. I will put enmity between you and the woman, and between your offspring and her offspring; he shall bruise your head, and you shall bruise his heel."

**Genesis 3:14-15 (ESV)**

What does this passage reveal about the ultimate destiny of the serpent?

_____
_____
_____
_____

### **Hebrews 2:14-16**

Who are the offspring of Abraham and the beneficiaries of Jesus' finished work on the Cross?

_____
_____
_____
_____

Read **Luke 12:49-53** – Jesus is called the "Prince of Peace", but this passage seems to present a starkly different message concerning Messiah. What are your thoughts?

_____
_____
_____

## A Call to Arms (1)

What does **John 5:19-24** reveal to us about the heart and mission of Jesus?

_____

_____

Read **John 6:37-40** and **Matthew 11:27**
What do these passages reveal to us about the mission of Jesus?

_____

_____

_____

What does **Hebrews 2:14-16** reveal to us about the nature of Spiritual warfare?

_____

_____

_____

_____

Unlike World War II and every other human conflict, the outcome of our Spiritual war is not in question. We do not fight "for" victory; we fight "because" we are already victorious.

War was declared in the Garden of Eden. Victory was secured at the Cross, but the battles continue to rage. For each and every Christian, neutrality is not an option. Every Christian is engaged in Spiritual warfare. Our mission is to serve the Lord of the mission.

| The Mission

## **Eternal Perspective (1.3)**

The Pharisees would have been very familiar with **Isaiah 61:1-3**. What does this passage reveal about the mission and purpose of the promised Messiah?

_____

_____

_____

In **Luke 4:17-20** what is the significance of Jesus' bold proclamation?

_____

_____

**Matthew 5:17-20**
What does Jesus reveal about his position in light of history, the nature and relevance of the "Old Testament", and his purpose on Earth?

_____

_____

_____

_____

People often misunderstand the word "prophecy" when it is properly applied from God's revealed word. Prophecies about Christ were not "predictions" about the future that were scattered throughout the pages of the Old Testament. These prophecies were God's revelation of his perfect plan and promise that are critical to his overall plan of redemption.

Prophets did not "predict the future". They revealed God's plan that would be carried out down to the smallest detail.

A Call to Arms (1)

## **Counter-Cultural (1.4)**

Instead of a conquering leader, John the Baptist described Jesus as the "Lamb of God" (**John 1:29**), and in **John 3:17,** we learn that He came with a message of redemption – not conquest.

In **Mark 2:15-17**, the Pharisees are shocked that Jesus would be seen sitting among sinners.

In **Matthew 20:25-27** and **Mark 10:42-45** we learn that Jesus' leadership style was rooted in serving others in stark contrast of what a worldly leader would be expected to do.

Picture the image of **Matthew 21:5-11**. How would this look in contrast to our view of a "conquering king"?

_____

_____

_____

**In John 18:33-37**, Jesus reveals the nature of his kingdom to Pilate. How would you describe this kingdom in your own words?

_____

_____

How do these passages speak to the mission of Jesus, in light of the world's expectations of the coming Messiah?

_____

_____

_____

_____

| The Mission

## Special Orders (1.5)

**Prepare for War**

The events leading up to World War II were widely evident with events dating back to 1931. It was only a matter of time until the enemy brought America into its conflict. America tried to ignore the inevitable and was caught off guard.

Every true follower of Christ is under attack from Spiritual enemies. Neutrality is not an option. As Believers we cannot be so naïve to expect to stay out of the spiritual war that the enemy has planned for us.

> "Unless we know the enemy we face and how to defeat him, our efforts to live out the Gospel are for naught. Scripture lists our main enemies as the world, the flesh and the devil, all of whom are formidable indeed"
> **R.C. Sproul** [3]

> "Beloved in our dearest Lord, Christ, the Scripture, your own hearts, and Satan's devices are the four prime things that should be first and most studied and searched. If any cast off study of these, they cannot be safe here, nor happy hereafter. It is my work as a Christian, but much more as a Watchman, to do my best to discover the fullness of Christ, the emptiness of the creature and the snares of the great deceiver"
> **Thomas Brooks** [4]

The messages are clear. Believers are called to be aware of our spiritual enemies and be prepared to engage the battles that are inevitable in the Christian life.

---

[3] Sproul, R.C., Tabletalk Magazine, September 2011, Ligonier Ministries

[4] Brooks, Thomas, *Precious Remedies Against Satan's Devices*, Carlisle, Pa. Banner of Truth Trust, 1652

# A Call to Arms (1)

**Spiritual War**

World War II was truly a global war, fought on multiple continents by enemy combatants with different methods and objectives.

The Christian war is not "global". Although we see a battlefield on earth, the real war is fought in the heavenly realms. Our mission is set. Our Leader is perfect and victory is certain.

**"If God is your co-pilot, change seats!"** We laugh when we see the bumper-sticker as we acknowledge the truth that phrase embodies. But, as a practical matter have you ever contemplated the depth of this very serious message and how powerful it can and should be in the life of every Believer?

**Wrong Seats**

In practice, the Christian business owner's primary goal is to grow and make a profit while asking God to stand at his side. As husbands we seek to love and serve our wives **with God's help**. As a worker, we do the best job we can and ask **God to help us** do it in a manner pleasing to Him.

On the golf course, we seek to shoot the lowest scores and pray that God will keep us from losing our temper when the ball lands in the water. In sharing Christ with others, we seek to be persuasive while **asking God to bless our efforts**. In our personal finances, we seek to handle our money, save for retirement and enjoy some of life's pleasures while we ask **God to help** us be better stewards of our money.

Notice the common element here? Even when we attempt to serve God, most of us will employ the weapons and strategies of the enemy: the world, the flesh and the devil, to accomplish our goals and objectives, while **we invite God along for the ride**.

If we truly want to "change seats", our mission and objectives have to change. If the objective and focus is to glorify God in everything we do, we have to completely change our perspective and be willing to **submit** to God in every respect.

## The Mission

Later in this study we will meet four Hebrew teenagers who lived their lives precisely that way. They did everything for the glory of God and completely disregarded the temporal consequences of their decisions. They left those in God's hands.

**Altered Perspectives**

As business owners, we should start with a plan that serves God above all else. If that results in a profit, we learn to use that profit to glorify Him. If we "fail" on the world's terms, we learn to use that failure to glorify God.

As salesmen, we should live to glorify God. If that results in a successful sale, we take the opportunity to use our success for His glory. If the sale falls through, we praise God because we trust His plan.

The same is true with our relationships with our wives and our children. The same is true in our leisure and recreational activities. Spiritual battlefields are fought with God at the center.

All too often we attempt to glorify God while living by the standards of the world, the flesh and Satan. God is relegated to the right seat (or the baggage compartment) in case we need him.

Jesus came to earth on a mission, and that mission was evident in everything he did and everything he said while he walked among us. Our mission is to serve the Lord of the mission.

How can we, as followers of Christ, become more focused on the eternal mission without being distracted by material possessions, conflicts, adversity, and other things that we face on a day to day basis?

## Truman (2)

"The historic fact remains, and must be judged in the after-time, that the decision whether or not to use the atomic bomb to compel the surrender of Japan was never an issue. There was unanimous, automatic, unquestioned agreement around our table; nor did I ever hear the slightest suggestion that we should do otherwise"

**Winston Churchill** [5]

In 1945, President Harry S. Truman was surrounded by advisors including British Prime Minister Winston Churchill, Henry Stinson (Secretary of War) Dwight Eisenhower, Douglas MacArthur, Admiral William Leahy, and others. But make no mistake, President Truman was faced with a decision that only he could make. He alone was responsible for making the final call.

Many modern historians have questioned America's decision to drop the atomic bombs on Hiroshima and Nagasaki. Those acts killed many innocent men, women and children living on Japanese soil. The destruction was horrific and the long-term effect was devastating.

---

[5] McCullough, David, *Truman*, Simon & Schuster, New York 1992

# The Mission

### Iwo Jima (February-March 1945 – 36 days)
- U.S. Marines killed – 6,800
- Japanese killed – 18,000
- Preferring death over surrender, only 216 Japanese were actually captured.

### Okinawa (April-June 1945 – 82 Days)
- Americans killed – 20,195
- Japanese killed – 77,000 – 110,000 (estimated)
- Civilian casualties – more than 150,000
- Japanese suicides – 2,000
- (Including Japanese General Ushijima Mitsuru, who chose suicide over the disgrace of surrender)

### Potsdam Declaration
### 26 July 1945
Truman, Churchill and Chinese President Chiang Kai-shek issued an ultimatum to Japan calling for its complete and unconditional surrender. The ultimatum stated that, if Japan did not surrender it would face "prompt and utter destruction"

In a widely broadcast speech picked up by Japanese news agencies, Truman warned the Japanese people that failure to accept the terms of the Potsdam Declaration would result in a:
"rain of ruin from the air, the like of which has
never been seen on earth".

Japanese Prime Minister Suzuki went to the Japanese press and reiterated his government's commitment to **ignore the Allies' demands and fight on**.

### Truman's Dilemma
In the aftermath of heavy casualties at Okinawa and Iwo Jima, one would have expected the Japanese to give up the fight. But the Japanese rejection of the Potsdam Declaration made it clear that surrender was not an option.

## Truman (2)

Truman's only alternative was the protraction of an already long and deadly war with the Japanese. That protraction would almost certainly be continued on the main island of Japan and the result would be the death of many more Americans and Japanese - including many civilians.

Advocates of using the bomb saw evidence that, although Japan was losing the war, they were no closer to surrender. The battle for Okinawa resulted in the loss of more than 13,000 troops as late as June, 1945. In spite of their losses, Japan showed no signs of surrender. Because of this, it was clear that an all-out invasion of Japan would be necessary and costly in terms of U.S. casualties. There were no easy alternatives.

### Truman's Decision

Truman's decision was carried out on 6 August 1945 when the Enola Gay took off on a mission that would have long term, devastating consequences. That mission marked the first time that atomic weapons were used in warfare. Two days later, a second atomic bomb was detonated over Nagasaki, setting the stage for the surrender of Japan and the end of World War II.

> "Truman made the correct choice in a difficult situation. Faced with the possibility of massive loss of life, conservatively estimated at 800,000 to 1,000,000 Americans alone, as well as with Japan's suicidal determination to defend the home islands in the face of an Allied invasion, Truman and his advisors realized that only a dramatic move could break this stalemate. The sudden destruction of two cities, however horrifying, seemed better than an extended campaign that would certainly kill millions of military personnel from both sides, as well as countless Japanese civilians"
>
> **Paul Walker** [6]

---

[6] Walker, Paul, *Truman's Dilemma: Invasion or The Bomb*, Pelican Publishing, Gretna, La 2003

| The Mission

"The final decision of where and when to use the atomic bomb was up to me. Let there be no mistake about it. I regarded the bomb as a military weapon and never had any doubt it should be used"

**President Harry S. Truman** [7]

## Commander in Chief

It is easy to second-guess President Truman, America's Commander in Chief, in his decision to deploy forces and how and where to take military action. President Truman and his advisors did not know how Japan would respond to the bombing of Hiroshima and Nagasaki. Even with the best advisors and the best intentions, our President was working with incomplete information and imperfect wisdom.

Even with the use of the atomic weapons deployed at Hiroshima and Nagasaki, the President had no way of knowing for certain how the Japanese would respond. He made his choice with the best information and wisdom he had at the time.

Like the Japanese, our spiritual enemies have no intention of ever surrendering. It is a battle to the finish.

However, as followers of Christ we know that the outcome of this war is not in doubt. We can serve our Commander in Chief in complete confidence. His wisdom and his plans are perfect, and he has the power to carry us to the victory celebration.

---

[7] McCullough, David, *Truman,* Simon & Schuster, New York 1992

Truman (2)

# Infinite Power (2.1)

"(God's) power, I must not forget to say, as a gathering up of the whole, is infinite. Power in the creature must have a limit for the creature itself is finite, but power in the Creator has neither measure nor bound. I am sure, beloved, **we treat our God often as though he were like ourselves**. We sit down after some one defeat or disappointment, and we say we will never try again—we suppose the work allotted to us to be impossible of performance. Is anything too hard for the Lord? Why limit ye the Holy One of Israel?"

**Charles Spurgeon** [8]

As a practical matter, our sincere theological beliefs don't always show up in the way we live out our Christian faith. Consider Spurgeon's statement and comment on the way you view God in your daily walk:

"..we treat our God often as though he were like ourselves"

"..power in the Creator has neither measure nor bound"

"Why limit ye the Holy One of Israel"

---

[8] Spurgeon, C. H.- Spurgeon's Sermons: Volume 12 (electronic ed.). Logos Library System; Albany, Oregon, 1998

| The Mission

## **Indescribable (2.2)**

"'There is no maverick molecule if God is sovereign.' If He cannot control the tiniest bits of the universe, then we cannot trust Him to keep His word."

**R.C. Sproul** [9]

From the following passages, comment on the boundaries (limits) on God's sovereignty:

**John 11:43** _____
**Matthew 28:1-10** _____
**Matthew 9:18-25** _____

_____

**Job 1:6-12** _____
**Matthew 8:28-32** _____
**Revelation 20:1-3** _____

_____

**Daniel 4:24-37** _____

_____

**Matthew 8:23-27** _____
**Exodus 14:21-25** _____

_____

**Isaiah 45:5-13** _____

_____

What part of the Universe is
beyond the sovereign power of God? _____

_____

_____

[9] Sproul, R.C., "God's Sovereignty" Tabletalk Magazine, February 22, 2007

Truman (2)

## **Perfect Wisdom (2.3)**

"God, the great Creator of all things, doth uphold, direct, dispose, and govern all creatures, actions, and things, from the greatest even to the least, by his most wise and holy providence, according to his infallible foreknowledge, and the free and immutable counsel of his own will, to the praise of the glory of his wisdom, power, justice, goodness, and mercy"

**Westminster Confession of Faith**

What do these passages say about God's wisdom ?

**Isaiah 40:25-31** _____

**Romans 11:32-36** _____

**Ephesians 3:7-11** _____

**Psalm 33:8-11** _____

"Let us listen then to the voice of the Lord, for he hath declared the secret; he hath revealed to the sons of men wherein true wisdom lieth, and we have it in the text, 'whoso trusteth in the Lord, happy is he;' and that sentence is put in conjunction with another which teaches us this truth, that to handle a matter wisely is to find good, and **the true way to handle a matter wisely is to trust God**. This is the short and brief method of escaping the greatest difficulties: this is the clue to the most intricate labyrinths; this is the lever which shall lift the most tremendous weights. He that trusts in the Lord has found out the way to handle matters wisely, and happy is he."

**Charles Spurgeon** [10]

---

[10] Spurgeon, Charles H.., "*Trust in God*", Sermon No 392, May 12, 1861, Metropolitan Tabernacle

| The Mission

## **Special Orders (2.4)**

There is a widespread belief that the Christian faith is blind and, to believe we are called to ignore any "rational" arguments against our faith. Indeed, many have come to Christ with a simple, child-like faith without the skepticism of a thousand questions.

However, the idea that faith in Christ is an act that requires suspension of rational thought is a myth perpetrated by men and women who are blinded by their own desire to deny the existence of a sovereign God. In light of Creation, to deny the existence of God is an irrational act of stubborn defiance. It is not the "rational" mind that rejects God. It is the defiant heart.

Many "skeptics" have investigated the claims of Christ and have found them to be true. Many have investigated the critics' challenges to Scripture. Many have investigated the geological and scientific evidence. Many have studied the historical challenges to the Bible. Indeed, many have found Christ through a process that began with skeptical curiosity – the complete opposite of "blind faith".

Study Scripture from the first words of Genesis to the final "Amen" in Revelation 22 and you will find a treasure-trove of information revealing God's character and personality. Read it. Meditate on it. Investigate the claims of God, Christ, and the Bible.

Today's average Christian is biblically "illiterate" compared to Christians of previous generations. The advent of the internet, social media, and the images and information that comes into our homes from a 52" device in our living rooms have replaced the Bible as a primary resource in our lives.

The result has been a re-definition of God from the real God described in Scripture to a "god" that is more like we want him to be. The "acceptable" character traits of God are highlighted and the parts of His character that are less to our liking are minimized or rejected altogether. The result is an imagined "God" who is like one of us.

## Truman (2)

The only problem is that, if you tend to view God as "one of us", you will find your god in the mirror, with all of the blemishes, warts and weaknesses that are part of the human existence. Faith in that "god" is not blind, but it most certainly is irrational. That "god" needs a natural explanation for every event in eternity and is subject to a wisdom that is far from perfect.

Scripture reveals the nature and personality of God. He is the author of His creation – not subject to or governed by it. Every molecule in the Universe was created by God and it is perfectly rational to believe he can control it.

God is sovereign over all things. God's power is infinite. His wisdom is unsearchable and his love is matchless. Every molecule in the Universe is under his sovereign control and, although we may not understand his reasons or his plans, it is perfectly rational and reasonable to trust him in everything and in every situation in life.

Among Christians however, the question is not usually one of intellectual assent. It is a question of the heart. Del Tackett, who produced "The Truth Project" (Focus on the Family) posed the question:

**"Do you really believe that what you believe is really real?"**

| The Mission

## Heads of State (3)

Most of us should be aware that World War II consisted of the Allied Powers (Britain, France, Canada, United States, and the Soviet Union), against the Axis Powers (Germany, Italy and Japan).

In truth there were many more nations who comprised each side of the conflict, and each nation (with their leadership) entered the war with different motivations and objectives.

The British presence included other nations in the United Kingdom, including Canada, Australia, New Zealand and South Africa. The Philippines were invaded by Japan early in the war and their soldiers fought alongside American troops throughout the Pacific. China had been at war with Japan since 1937, but did not officially become an ally until 1941. The United States did not enter the war until she was attacked by Japan and the Soviet Union did not join the war until Germany attacked the USSR in 1941.

Also included in the list of "Allies" were Poland and France, who were both defeated prior to America's entrance into the war. Other Allied countries occupied by Nazi Germany included Belgium, Greece, the Netherlands, Norway, Czechoslovakia and Luxemburg.

The aggressors (Axis Powers) in World War II included Nazi Germany (Adolf Hitler), Italy (Benito Mussolini), and Japan (Emperor Hirohito). Each of these had different motivations for engaging in the war.

Heads of State (3)

## Hirohito

Hirohito was emperor of Japan from 1926 until his death in 1989. After the war, He portrayed himself as a constitutional monarch with very little power who allowed his military leaders to take him to war.

Whether or not this portrayal is appropriate, during World War II, Japan attacked nearly all of its Asian neighbors, allied itself with Nazi Germany and launched a surprise assault on the U.S. naval base at Pearl Harbor, with an almost simultaneous attack on the Philippines.

In order to meet their economic needs in the wake of the Great Depression, Japanese leaders felt that Asian colonies could supply them with raw materials and aid them in their economic problems through conquest.

Following the Japanese attacks on Manchuria and Mongolia America rescinded its commercial treaty with the Empire of Japan and began to restrict essential shipments of oil and metal. By 1941 the U.S. had joined in a full embargo that restricted Japanese access to oil.

## Pierre Laval

When France fell to Germany, it was separated into two parts: occupied France, directly governed by the Nazis; and Vichy France, which was run by hand-picked puppets of Germany.

French Prime Minister Pierre Laval would ultimately be remembered as a traitor conspiring with the Nazis during their occupation of France while he was the effective political head of unoccupied Vichy France.

Laval was made Chief Minister of Vichy France in April 1942, where he remained until 1944. He, along with Marshal Petain and others gained reputations as collaborators with Berlin. At the end of the war Laval was tried, convicted, and executed for treason.

| The Mission

Many historians see Laval as an opportunist who joined the Nazi effort for reasons of personal aspiration. There are others who saw him as attempting to protect France from the devastation that Hitler had inflicted on Germany.

## Neville Chamberlain

History has not been kind to British Prime Minister Neville Chamberlain. His failed attempt to negotiate "peace through appeasement" with Hitler in the Munich Agreement in 1938 was his most notable act as Prime Minister.

Despite the outcome, Chamberlain was motivated by a passionate desire for peace. He sincerely believed that Hitler would cease his aggressions if the world would meet his demands.

It was Chamberlain who ultimately called for a declaration of war against Germany in September of 1939. He resigned as Prime Minister in 1940 and was succeeded by Winston Churchill.

**3 September 1939**
Following the invasion of Poland, Prime Minister Neville Chamberlain gave Germany an ultimatum to withdraw from Poland. His announcement came at 11:15 am:
**"this country is at war with Germany"**

## Winston Churchill

British Prime Minister Winston Churchill was arguably one of the strongest leaders in World War II. He disagreed vehemently with Chamberlain. He never trusted Hitler and saw the war as an unavoidable reality.

Churchill and Chamberlain were both motivated by their love of country. One chose a path that eventually led to victory, the other will be remembered primarily for his failure.

Heads of State (3)

## Franklin Roosevelt

Franklin Delano Roosevelt was the only American President to have been elected to four (4) terms in office. He was America's President before the outbreak of World War II and served until his death in 1945, shortly before the war ended.

Most historians credit his leadership, working with Churchill, as being a critical factor in the defeat of German and Japanese aggression. Roosevelt took an active role in strategic decisions in the prosecution of the war working with and through his military advisers and took an active role in choosing the principal field commanders and in making decisions regarding wartime strategy.

## Leadership

No one can go inside the minds of these world leaders. Even the best leaders have underlying motivations that we may never understand.

Hitler and Mussolini were megalomaniacal narcissists. Hirohito was motivated by economics. Stalin responded in defense of his country. Roosevelt, Churchill and Chamberlain acted out of love for their country.

As Christians, we serve a perfect Leader whose motivations are revealed in his character and are beyond human comprehension. God is just, and his justice is perfect. God is also perfect in his love – as evidenced in his mercy, his grace, his providence, and his willingness to send his Son to the Cross for people completely undeserving of his love.

The Mission

## **Perfect Love (3.1)**

"Yes Jesus Loves Me, Yes Jesus Loves Me
Yes Jesus Loves Me –
For the Bible Tells Me So"[11]

Do you really believe that statement?
  "God has blessed me with a great family, a job, a home…
  …… Yes, Jesus loves me"

Do you still believe that when:
- Your child is born with a congenital abnormality;
- Your husband or wife walks out on you;
- You are diagnosed with a terminal disease;
- You are forced into bankruptcy or sued by someone?

Do you believe that God's love was perfect and present:
- When the towers fell on September 11th;
- In Katrina or the Tsunami;
- At Auschwitz during the Holocaust?

How do the following passages reflect on the statement that "God is Love"

**John 3:16** _____
**Psalm 33:18-22** _____
**I John 3:1-3** _____
**I John 3:16** _____
**I John 4:7-12** _____

_____
_____

---

[11] Public Domain. Based on a poem by Anna Bartlett Warner, with Lyrics added by William Bradbury – Biography and hymns of Anna Bartlett Warner (1827-1915)

Heads of State (3)

# Unimaginable Love (3.2)

Even non-Christians like to think that "God is love", without truly understanding the definition of that word. God loves unlovable people. He loves sinners who regularly rebel against Him and who continuously demand their own way. In short, he loves you and me – in spite of the fact that we are totally undeserving of that love.

Read **John 19** and comment on God's love

_____

_____

_____

_____

Who put Jesus on the Cross? Herod certainly played a role. The religious leaders who should have recognized him as Messiah demanded his death. Roman soldiers under the command of Pontius Pilate carried out the execution. Even the Jewish people called for his death, preferring Barabbas. One of the interesting points about the crucifixion of Christ is that so many people who held opposing views on life and ideology were able to come together to agree on this one issue – Jesus deserved to die.

Jews, Romans, and Gentiles all contributed to Christ's death. Ultimately we, as Christians, are guilty of the blood of Christ. It was our own sin that put him on the Cross.

Yet with all of the culpable parties that bear responsibility for Jesus' death on the Cross, there is one and only one Person who put Christ on that Cross. That was God himself. He put His Son on the Cross as evidence of his unimaginable and unfathomable love for you and me.

"For God so loved the world...." John 3:16

| The Mission

## **Amazing in Grace (3.3)**

"Mercy" is defined as not receiving the punishment we deserve. "Grace" is defined as receiving a reward that we have not earned. We love to sing "Amazing Grace" in our churches on Sunday morning. But do we really understand how amazing God's grace truly is?

When we were mired in our own depravity, God called us to himself. But He did not stop there. He sanctifies us by his grace and he sustains our faith by his grace. We could not and did not earn it or deserve it. His grace was and continues to be a gift that God provides as further evidence of his love for us.

Read **Ephesians 2:8-10**
reflecting on these four words

**Works**

**Workmanship**

**Gift**

**Boast**

Let's face it. From Billy Graham to Mother Teresa, Moses to the Apostles, to the waitress at Waffle House to you and me – Our problem and its solution are the same: We are all sinners in need of a gracious Savior.

You don't have to preach, teach, attend seminary, or learn Greek. You don't have to go to Africa or even door-to-door to share your faith. God set the bar so high, it could only be satisfied through his righteous Son, and yet so low, that each of us could meet him through faith in his Son.

Grace is the ultimate evidence of God's perfect love.

Heads of State (3)

## **Rich in Mercy (3.4)**

As grace is the gift we do not deserve, mercy is what happens when we do not have to pay the price (penalty) for what we do deserve. When we turn our lives over to Christ, his perfect righteousness is imputed to us (grace) and our record of sin is credited to Him (mercy).

**2 Corinthians 5:17-21** – Just how high was the price Jesus paid for our salvation?

**Matthew 27:45-46**

Jesus had never known sin. God could not bear to look on his sin-soaked Son who became my sin and your sin so that God could look on us and see us clothed in righteousness.

Zechariah, father of John the Baptist, was given a prophecy, recorded in **Luke 1:67-79**. Read what he says about Jesus in verses 76-79. How is God's love revealed in his mercy toward us?

> "The mercy of the heart of God
> is to be seen in the remission of sin, and in the
> visitation of his love when he comes to us
> as "the dayspring from on high.
> Great is the tenderness of divine mercy."
> **Charles Spurgeon**

## Special Orders (3.5)

As human parents, our love for our children is less than perfect, our wisdom is flawed and our control over their circumstances is limited.

As Christians we have a Heavenly Father without those limitations. His perfect wisdom, limitless love and complete sovereignty exist in perfect harmony and without contradiction, so that in every situation and circumstance our complete faith is perfectly reasonable and rational.

## Perfect Faith Triad

- **God is completely sovereign** – from the hairs on your head, to the stars in the sky, from the tiniest sparrow to kings and princes, from the forces of nature to the actions of Satan himself.

- **God's love is perfect** –He is the very definition of love (1 John 4:7-8). His mercy and grace are the manifestations of that love and, since we have earned neither of them, neither can be taken away.

- **God is infinitely wise** – he cannot make a mistake. While he is not the author of our sin and he is not the author of evil, all the evil that the world, flesh and devil can conjure and even our most grievous sins never catch him by surprise.

When we are faced with a trial or pain, there is a voice inside who tells us that "God doesn't love you", or "God is not in control". That voice is the voice of the enemy.

Heads of State (3)

# Axis Powers

"Unless we know the enemy
we face and how to defeat him,
our efforts to live out the Gospel
are for naught.

"Scripture lists our main enemies
as the world, the flesh and the Devil
*(1 John 2:15-17; Galatians 5:16;
1 Peter 5:8),*
all of whom are formidable indeed"
**R.C. Sproul** [12]

---

[12] Sproul, R.C., Table Talk Magazine, September 2011, Ligonier Ministries, Sanford, FL.

| Axis Powers

# The Big Lie (4)

"Through clever and constant application of propaganda, people can be made to see paradise as hell, and also the other way around, to consider the most wretched sort of life as paradise"

**Adolf Hitler**

"in the big lie there is always a certain force of credibility; because the broad masses of a nation are always more easily corrupted in the deeper strata of their emotional nature than consciously or voluntarily; and thus in the primitive -simplicity of their minds they more readily fall victims to the big lie than the small lie, since they themselves often tell small lies in little matters but would be ashamed to resort to large-scale falsehoods"

**Adolph Hitler**
Mein Kampf

Today we remember him as a monster – one of the evilest men in all of history. But, to learn from history, we must remember how he ascended to power – not as the monster, but as the charismatic heroic leader offering great promises to those who would follow him.

The Big Lie (4)

**Adolf Hitler**
He was born in Braunau, Austria on 20 April 1889.

He was one of the most charismatic and deceptive leaders in all of history. His own words tell the story of how he convinced the German people to follow him into a bloody world war and the mass genocide of what he called "inferior" races of people.

**The "Prophet"**

"In the course of my life I have very often been a prophet, and have usually been ridiculed for it. During the time of my struggle for power, it was in the first instance only the Jewish race that received my prophecies with laughter when I said that I would one day take over the leadership of the state and with it that of the whole nation and that I would then among other things settle the Jewish problem...but I think that for some time now they have been laughing on the other side of their face. Today I will once more be a prophet: if the international Jewish financiers in and outside Europe should succeed in plunging the nations once more into a world war, then the result will not be the Bolshevizing of the earth and thus the victory of Jewry, but the annihilation of the Jewish race in Europe!".

**Adolf Hitler**
Speech to the Reichstag – 30 January 1939

**Christianity**

"I shall never come personally to terms with the Christian lie. Our epoch in the next 200 years will certainly see the end of the disease of Christianity. My regret will have been that I couldn't behold its demise"

**Adolph Hitler**, 27 February 1942[13]

"It is deplorable that the Bible should have been translated into German, and that the whole of German Folk should have thus become exposed to this Jewish mumbo jumbo"

**Adolf Hitler,** 4 April 1942

---

[13] Trevor-Roper, Hugh ed (2000), Hitler's Table Talk 1941-1944, Enigma Books, New York

"What is this God who takes pleasure only in seeing men grovel before him?"
**Adolf Hitler,** 11 November 1941

"It is a great pity that this tendency towards religious thought can find no better outlet than the Jewish pettifoggery of the Old Testament. For religious people who, in the solitude of winter, continually seek ultimate light on their religious problems with the assistance of the Bible, must eventually become spiritually deformed. The wretched people strive to exact truths from these Jewish chicaneries, where in fact no truths exist"
**Adolf Hitler** ,4 April 1942

Let no one deceive you into believing that Adolf Hitler was a Christian nor that the Nazi cause had any Christian roots. He saw the Bible as a compilation of myths and Jewish propaganda. He expressed outward distain for the Apostle Paul who, in his mind, distorted the message of Jesus. As for Jesus himself, Hitler was adamant in denying Jesus' virgin birth and his Jewish roots.

Hitler tolerated the organized churches in Germany as a means of controlling the people. While he sought to annihilate the Jews and Gypsies, he worked to control the message of the Church and use it for his Nazi propaganda.

He was successful in the "nazification" of a portion of the organized Church. The ones who resisted were imprisoned or killed.

**"Nazi"**
In February, 1920 the National Socialist German Worker's Party, later nicknamed "Nazi" published its program for wealth redistribution, nationalization of trusts, free education and other socialist reforms – but rights reserved only for German citizens.

Hitler seduced the people with his personality and his charisma. But he used force to maintain his power. His Gestapo and the Schutzstaffel (S.S.) were tasked with the responsibility of

## The Big Lie (4)

eliminating any and all opposition to the Nazi regime. Anyone suspected of being disloyal were arrested and imprisoned or executed.

What could possibly have caused the German people to fall for his seduction? For all of the books written on the subject, the simplest and most plausible answer is that the German people were beaten, exhausted, and hungry. Their national pride was decimated in the aftermath of World War I and their misery was exacerbated by the Great Depression.

### Treaty of Versailles (World War I)

The Treaty of Versailles signified a humiliating defeat for the German people. A once proud nation was demilitarized and forced pay reparations. Nationalism declined and the population felt betrayed by their government (Weimar Republic) for allowing the Treaty to pass.

In addition to financial penalties, Germany was forced to give up 13% of her territory and 10% of her population.

It was during this time that the German economy began to collapse, in part a consequence of World War I and the subsequent payment of reparations. Artificial inflation of the money supply ("quantitative easing") led to devaluation of the German Mark to the point where it was almost worthless – and that, in turn led to hyperinflation.

The Treaty of Versailles brought resentment and distrust of the German people for their own government. They were convinced that their financial woes were a direct result of the Treaty.

The German people felt humiliated and betrayed. Adolf Hitler offered hope for a better life and restoration of national pride. What he delivered was unimaginable devastation, cruelty, and bloodshed, not only to the Jews and "lesser races", but also to his own people and to millions of others who engaged him in battle.

**This "heroic leader" was, indeed, a monster.**

Axis Powers

# The Adversary (4.1)

"There are two equal and opposite errors into which our race can fall about the devils. One is to disbelieve in their existence. The other is to believe and to feel an excessive and unhealthy interest in them"-

**C.S. Lewis** [14]

He has been the subject of cartoons, books and movies. People worship him, fear him, laugh at him and deny his existence. He is depicted glamorously, vomiting pea soup, or as a Halloween character with horns and a pointed tail.

Satan is real. Scripture describes him in intricate detail. He was created as a celestial being who challenged God. He has a demonic host at his disposal and a world culture is his playground. Scripture tells us what Satan himself does not want us to know. Scripture tells us about the real "Satan", his power, his tactics, his schemes and his destiny.

He is called by many names:

| | |
|---|---|
| **Isaiah 14:12-13** | *Lucifer, Day Star* |
| **Luke 4:2** | *Devil, "Slanderer", Diablos* |
| **Ephesians 6:12** | *Prince of Darkness* |
| **Revelation 9:11** | *Abaddon/Apollyon (Destroyer)* |
| **Ephesians 2:2** | *Prince of the Power of the Air* |
| **Revelation 12:9** | *Serpent / Great Dragon* |
| **Revelation 12:10** | *Accuser* |
| **1 Peter 5:8** | *Adversary (Satan)* |
| **Matthew 12:24** | *Beelzebub – Lord of the flies* |
| **2 Corinthians 6:15** | *Belial(worthless, wicked)* |
| **John 8:44** | *Father of Lies* |

---

[14] Lewis, C.S. – *The Screwtape Letters*, C.S. Lewis Pte. Ltd. 1942

Warrior – Page 42

The Big Lie (4)

## **Seduction (4.2)**

"Christ, the Scripture, your own hearts, and Satan's devices are the four prime things that should be first and most studied and searched. If any cast off the study of these, they cannot be safe here or happy hereafter" [15]

**Thomas Brooks**

To the rest of the world, he is their king, their deliverer, their source of "happiness". Satan did not seize power over the world by force – he took it by seduction, deception, and empty promises. His power over the minds and actions of others is not rooted in fear and intimidation, but in his seductive nature over the hearts and minds of those who serve him.

**Ezekiel 28:11-19** – Satan's attributes:

Verse 12 _____

Verse 14 _____

Verse 15 _____

Verse 17 _____

Satan's followers were taken captive by deception and seduction. God has denied him access to the Believers' souls so he is ruthless in his efforts to render us ineffective in this world – **by any means necessary.**

As Believers, we should view Satan the same way we view Hitler; not as the German people saw him in 1935, but as an evil force to be taken seriously. **He is the Adversary.**

---

[15] Brooks, Thomas, *Precious Remedies Against Satan's Devices*, Carlisle, Pa. Banner of Truth Trust, 1652

Axis Powers

## **Father of Lies (4.3)**

**"Satan promises the best, but pays with the worst**; he promises honour, and pays with disgrace; he promises pleasure, and pays with pain; he promises profit, and pays with loss; he promises life, and pays with death. But God pays as he promises; all his payments are made in pure gold." [16]

**Thomas Brooks**

What do these passages reveal about Satan's methods and of his relationship to the world?

**2 Corinthians 4:1-6**
**John 8:41-47**

According to Brooks, what should we expect when we listen to Satan's promises?

"Satan's number one tactic is **deception**. As the Father of Lies, he is a deceiver and deluder. Part of his strategy is to blind our minds so we can't ascertain God's truth. He does this by feeding us lies about God, about ourselves, and about the world." [17]

**Chip Ingram**

---

[16] Brooks, Thomas, *Precious Remedies Against Satan's Devices*, Carlisle, Pa. Banner of Truth Trust, 1652

[17] Ingram, Chip, Living on the Edge, September 17, 2015

The Big Lie (4)

## **Tempter (4.4)**

"Most people want to be delivered
from temptation,
but they would like it to keep in touch"[18]

Satan's primary (but not only) mode of attack is through temptation. By causing a Christian to fall, he can inflict damage on him, his family, his reputation, his witness, and others around him. The damage can result in long-lasting consequences and render the Believer powerless in his service to Christ and to the Church.

What form do Satan's temptations take in the following passages

**Matthew 4:8-9** _____
**Genesis 3:1-5** _____

How should we respond?

**Romans 12:9-12** _____
**I Thessalonians 5:14-22** _____

**2 Corinthians 10:3-5** _____

"Until we have sinned, Satan is a parasite;
when we have sinned he is a tyrant"
**Thomas Brooks** [19]

---

[18] Author unknown
[19] Brooks, *Thomas, Precious Remedies against Satan's Devices*, Carlisle, Pa :The Banner of Truth Trust, 1652

## Special Orders (4.5)

True Believers are sealed by the Holy Spirit and our souls are beyond Satan's reach. The best he can hope for is to render us ineffective in our daily walk and our witness to others. In order to win the daily battles, we are called to be on guard for attacks from the world, the flesh and Satan's demonic army.

As we engage our spiritual enemies, it bears repeating the words of C.S. Lewis:

> "There are two equal and opposite errors into which our race can fall about the devils. One is to disbelieve in their existence. The other is to believe and to feel an excessive and unhealthy interest in them"-
> 
> **C.S. Lewis** [20]

On one end of the spectrum, there are those who treat the devil and demonic beings as "mythical metaphors" for the struggle between good and evil. On the other end of the spectrum are people that attempt to find a demonic spirit behind every trial and adversity in life.

C.S. Lewis reminds us to avoid both extremes. Scripture paints an accurate picture of who Satan is. He is real and the fallen angels who serve him are real. Satan is powerful and crafty. But Satan is an enemy that has already been defeated by the work of Christ on the Cross. Satan is no match for God.

Take another look at **Thomas Brooks** instruction (From *Precious Remedies Against Satan's Devices*):

> "Christ, the Scripture, your own hearts, and Satan's devices are the four prime things that should be first and most studied and searched. If any cast off the study of these, they cannot be safe here or happy hereafter"
> 
> **Thomas Brooks**

---

[20] Lewis, C.S. - *The Screwtape Letters*, C.S. Lewis Pte. Ltd. 1942

# The Big Lie (4)

Notice Brooks does not call us to study Satan – he calls us to study and understand his **devices**. He also encourages us to study Christ and the Scriptures while making sure our hearts are in the right place.

Satan's playbook is not complex, but his timing and application of his schemes are remarkable and he is quite adept at using it for his own purposes.

## Temptation

Satan's primary tactic is temptation that leads to moral failure which, in turn, hinders our testimony. The discouragement or despair that follows will make us want to give up in the fight. Adversity can lead to doubt. Then, when he has knocked us down – he is a relentless prosecutor. "You are guilty! You are unworthy! God can never forgive you! God can never use you!"

We should never toy with temptation. There is no reward or trophy to be gained in facing it – Scripture simply calls us to flee temptation.... In other words: Run Forrest!

> "Therefore let anyone who thinks that he stands take heed lest he fall. No temptation has overtaken you that is not common to man. God is faithful, and he will not let you be tempted beyond your ability, but with the temptation he will also provide the way of escape, that you may be able to endure it".
>
> **1 Corinthians 10:12-13**

## The Lie

As simple as it may sound, "truth" is the antidote to Satan's lies. Ephesians 6 reminds us to put on the "Belt of Truth". As a warrior in biblical times, the belt was the first weapon he would put on. That belt held the scabbard that carried the sword.

**Ephesians 6:17** says that the sword of the Spirit is the Word of God. The belt of truth and the sword of the Spirit are the only reliable and authoritative sources of truth in the universe –the only perfect antidote to Satan's lie.

# Axis Powers

Confronted by Pilate in John 18, Jesus told him "For this purpose I was born and for this purpose I have come into the world—to bear witness to the truth. Everyone who is of the truth listens to my voice." Pilate's response? "What is truth?"

> **John 8:31**
> "If you abide in my word, you are truly my disciples, and you will know the truth, and the truth will set you free."

There are no books, blogs, or websites – no preachers, teachers or motivational speakers who are adequate substitutes for God's Word. The antidote to Satan's lies is to be set free by abiding in the Word of God.

> "A man never gets anything out of the devil,
> even if he conquers him. You will find in combat with him that even if you win the victory, you come off with gashes and wounds of which you will carry the scars to your grave.
>
> 'All the while,' says Mr. Bunyan, while Christian was fighting with Apollyon, 'I did note that he did not so much as give one smile.' Oh no, there is nothing to smile about when the arch-enemy is upon us. He is such a master of the cruel art of soul-wounding that every stroke tells."
> **Charles Spurgeon** [21]

---

[21] Spurgeon, Charles H, - Peter's Restoration Sermon #2034

## Tojo (5)

Hideki Tojo was born in 1884 and executed for war crimes in 1948. He became Japan's Minister of War in 1940 and was appointed Prime Minister in October of 1941.

Tojo had expressed admiration for European dictators (notably Adolf Hitler). By the time he was appointed Prime Minister, Tojo was convinced that war with America could not be avoided. Deciding that a massive surprise attack would be sufficient to keep America out of the Pacific, he authorized the attack on Pearl Harbor

Tojo embraced a culture that believed that surrender was the most disgraceful thing a person could do. To be a prisoner of war was unthinkable and bordered on sub-human behavior.

For this reason, though the Japanese originally agreed to the Geneva Convention, the Convention was never ratified or acknowledged by Japanese leaders – including Tojo. He expected his soldiers to fight to the death (including suicide, if necessary) rather than suffer the disgrace of surrender.

Tojo's atrocious treatment of prisoners of war was rooted in his outright disgust toward anyone who would even entertain the idea of surrender. American and Filipino prisoners were seen as less than human and were subjected to unimaginable torture, beatings and starvation throughout the course of the war.

Axis Powers

## Casualties

The majority of Japan's battlefield successes occurred early in the war. As a consequence, a significant number of Allied prisoners of war were captured by 1942. This meant that most of these men had to survive in captivity for more than three (3) years. Not only was their internment lengthy, but they were also subjected to unimaginable brutality.

The mortality rate in a German prisoner of war camp was around 4%. **The mortality rate in a Japanese P.O.W. camp was 27%.**

Men were allowed to die from untreated diseases like pellagra, beriberi, diphtheria, scurvy, dysentery, cholera or dengue fever. Many prisoners (especially the weak) were executed by shootings, beheadings, and with bayonets. Some were buried alive and some were subjected to medical experimentation. Prisoners were often fed maggot infested rice and deprived of water or food for days. Disease and malnutrition were rampant among prisoners of war.

In an effort to cover up their atrocities, shortly before the end of the war, the Japanese carried out mass executions of prisoners of war.

Japan officially surrendered on 2 September 1945. Nine (9) days later, 11 September 1945, Hideki Tojo attempted suicide but survived a gunshot wound to his chest. Tojo was arrested and brought to trial for his war crimes in November of 1948. He was held responsible instigating Japan's aggressive foreign policy in the early 1940s and for the horrific abuse of prisoners of war in violation of the Geneva Convention.

Tojo (5)

## Bataan Death March

**9 April 1942 – Luzon, Philippines**

Approximately 75,000 Filipino and American prisoners of war were forced to make a 65-mile march over several days in intense heat while being deprived of water, subjected to beatings and executions along the way. Thousands perished in what became known as the **Bataan Death March**.

The Bataan Death March covered some 65 miles from Mariveles, on the southern end of the Bataan Peninsula, to San Fernando. The men were divided into groups of approximately 100 each, and it typically took each group around five days to complete the march. The exact casualty figures are unknown, but it is believed that thousands of troops died because of the brutality of their Japanese captors, who starved and beat the prisoners, and bayoneted those too weak to walk. Survivors were taken by rail from San Fernando to prisoner-of-war camps, where thousands more died as a result of disease, malnutrition, mistreatment and starvation.

## Beast of Bataan

Lieutenant General Masaharu Homma was commander of the Japanese invasion forces in the Philippines. He earned the nickname "Beast of Bataan". He was eventually held responsible for Japanese atrocities during the Bataan Death March. Japanese Emperor Hirohito stripped Homma of his military commission and revoked all of his medals for his involvement at Bataan.

After the war, an American military tribunal tried and convicted Homma for war crimes at Bataan. He was executed by firing squad on 3 April 1946.

| Axis Powers

Commenting on Homma's war crimes, General MacArthur is quoted:

> "If this defendant does not deserve his judicial fate, none in jurisdictional history ever did. There can be no greater, more heinous or more dangerous crime than the mass destruction, under guise of military authority or military necessity, of helpless men incapable of further contribution to war effort. A failure of law process to punish such acts of criminal enormity would threaten the very fabric of world society." [22]

## Bridge on the River Kwai

You may be familiar with the 1957 World War II movie, "Bridge on the River Kwai" that starred Alec Guinness and William Holden. The movie was loosely based on a real-life series of events where American and British prisoners of war were subjected to brutal treatment at the hands of their Japanese captors in World War II.

The real history of how the bridge was built was but a small part in the larger story of the construction of a railway between Burma and China During World War II. The original project was expected to take more than five (5) years but the Japanese used forced labor from Allied prisoners of war coupled with brutal treatment to complete the project in only 16 months.

The work on the railway went on 24 hours per day with prisoners who were required to work 12-18 hours per day. 69 men were beaten to death by Japanese guards. Most of the other casualties were from overwork, malnutrition and disease.

The majority of the work was done in jungle conditions where temperatures often exceeded 100 degrees (F) and humidity was incredibly high. Add to those conditions the existence of lice and

---

[22] Chen, Peter, Masaharu Homma, World War II Database, Lava Development, LLC, WW2db.com, 18 February 2009

other insects and it is hard to imagine a more horrific test of endurance.

In addition to the hard labor they endured, POWs were fed very poorly. Often it was rotten or maggot-infested rice. As a result, they contracted scurvy, pellagra and beriberi. POWs had to supplement their rations with whatever they could find, including scorpions, snakes, and rats. Sanitation conditions were also poor leading to cholera, dengue fever, diphtheria, and dysentery.

## Tojo's Legacy

While Nazi Germany is known for its horrific treatment of Jews during the Holocaust, allied prisoners of war in Germany received much better treatment than their counterparts in the Pacific theatre. Theirs was a hellish nightmare until the final shot was fired and the Japanese surrendered on 11 September 1945. Hideki Tojo deserves much of the credit for the treatment of Allied prisoners of war during World War II.

Tojo served as Japan's Minister of War from 22 July 1940 to 22 July 1944 and as Japanese Prime Minister from 17 October 1941 to 22 July 1944. He was a major voice in the Japanese decision to attack Pearl Harbor and he administered the policies that led to the poor treatment of prisoners of war.

In 1944, after suffering defeat at the Battle of the Philippine Sea, Tojo lost the confidence of the Emperor. Tojo was forced to resign as Prime Minister.

Hideki Tojo failed in his suicide attempt. As he was being attended, Japanese reporters recorded his words:

> "I am very sorry it is taking me so long to die. The Greater East Asia War was justified and righteous. .... I wait for the righteous judgement of history"

Indeed, the "righteous judgment of history" would remember him as the face of Japanese atrocities and as a war criminal deserving of death by hanging.

## **Unresolved Sin (5.1)**

*"Until we have sinned, Satan is a parasite; when we have sinned he is a tyrant"*
**Thomas Brooks** [23]

Satan and his emissaries do not have a complex set of plans with which they will attack the Christian. But make no mistake, the plans they have are effective. The primary weapon of the enemy is temptation. Satan has studied our tendencies and spiritual weaknesses and is adept at using our own flesh and a complicit world culture to lure us away from following Christ.

But temptation is only one of many devices (schemes) that he uses against us. After he has lured us into his trap, he uses a variety of schemes to keep us locked up in his prison cell; weak, disabled, defeated and ineffective as followers of Christ.

**How does Satan use even the "smallest" sins against us?**
"A certain man wanted to sell his house for $2,000. Another man wanted very badly to buy it, but because he was poor, he couldn't afford the full price. After much bargaining, the owner agreed to sell the house for half the original price with just one stipulation: he would retain ownership of one small nail protruding from just over the door.

"After several years, the original owner wanted the house back, but the new owner was unwilling to sell. So the first owner went out, found the carcass of a dead dog, and hung it from the single nail he still owned. Soon the house became unlivable, and the family was forced to sell the house to the owner of the nail.

"The Haitian pastor's conclusion: If we leave the Devil with even one small peg in our life, he will return to hang his rotting garbage on it, making it unfit for Christ's habitation."
**Haitian Parable**

---

[23] Brooks, Thomas, *Precious Remedies against Satan's Devices* Carlisle, Pa., The Banner of Truth Trust, 1652

## Tojo (5)

What are the inherent dangers in ignoring or dismissing sins in our own lives?

_____
_____
_____
_____
_____

All sin carries consequences. There are sins for which there are little or no natural consequences and there are sins that naturally carry much more severe consequences in life. There are times when we deserve more than we get and other times when it seems that the consequences feel "unfair" from a human perspective.

But even the smallest **sins** have the capacity to snowball out of control making us wonder "how did it go this far?". So-called minor sins can multiply and build on one another, taking us to a place we never expected to go.

The choice to ignore any sin has the potential to take you farther than you ever expected to go, keep you longer than you ever expected to stay, and cost you far more than you ever expected to pay.

The Haitian pastor has a message for all of us:

**There is rotting garbage on your doorpost. Take it down.... better yet, get rid of the nail!**

| Axis Powers

## **Nip it in the Bud (5.2)**

The enemy has the capacity to take us down a path from temptation to painful captivity / bondage. While Christ has promised ultimate victory, even true Believers are not immune from following Satan deep into his prison.

The path to spiritual captivity normally begins with temptation and a choice. Each additional step in the devolution toward captivity becomes more difficult.

Comment on Saul's choices, decisions, and consequences in these passages:

**1 Samuel 13:2-14**
**1 Samuel 14:14-45**
**1 Samuel 25**

When Saul was first anointed king, he demonstrated great humility. After he tasted temporal "success", his humility was replaced by jealousy, pride, impatience, envy, and anger.

God spoke to Saul through Samuel but he would not listen. So God gave him over to his own desires and anointed David as his replacement. Saul made choices that directly contradicted God's commands. Those choices cost him his throne, his life, and ultimately, his relationship with God.

In the words of that great theologian Barney Fife, our first and best choice in dealing with sin and Satan is to "Nip it! Nip it in the bud!"

Warrior – Page 56

Tojo (5)

# **Grieving the Spirit (5.3)**

"Satan's first device to draw the soul into sin is to present the bait—and hide the hook; to present the golden cup—and hide the poison; to present the sweet, the pleasure, and the profit that may flow in upon the soul by yielding to sin—and to hide from the soul the wrath and misery that will certainly follow the committing of sin"

**Thomas Brooks**

Scripture promises that we are sealed by the Holy Spirit. Yet, read the following passage concerning Saul. Is this relevant today?

**1 Samuel 16:14-16**

_____
_____
_____
_____
_____

Every Believer is gifted with the indwelling of the Holy Spirit. It is He who provides the light of understanding to allow us hear the word of God as revealed in Scripture.

It is His voice speaking to us when we are tempted and when we sin. It is His voice that encourages us when we stumble. It is His voice that comforts us when we are hurting.

When we close our eyes, ears and hearts to the voice of the Holy Spirt, we are guilty of resisting, quenching or grieving the Spirit. These three terms have different meanings, but all refer to our turning away from His protection and His guidance to seek our own way. And we do that to our own peril.

We are called to listen and respond to the Spirit when He speaks into our lives.

Axis Powers

## **From Parasite to Tyrant (5.4)**

After he has lured us into his snare through temptation, Satan works to hold us through guilt and discouragement by reminding us of our moral failures. His goal is alienation from God – too guilty to repent; to evil to pray; to filthy to be in God's presence.

In **Psalm 51**, David said "I know my transgressions and my sin is ever before me", and in **Psalm 32** he cries out in desperation "when I kept silent, my bones wasted away through my groaning all day long".

**Zechariah 3:1-5** _____

**Romans 8:1-3** _____

_____

For Christians, the voice of guilt and condemnation is from the enemy. Guilt leads to despair. The Holy Spirit brings conviction that leads to repentance and forgiveness at the foot of the cross.

Satan uses guilt to turn you away from Christ. When the Holy Spirit speaks to your sin, he is calling you to respond by turning back to Christ. The remedy for shame and despair is found in the blessing of repentance.

*"When Satan tempts me to despair,*
*and tells me of the guilt within,*
*upward I look and see him there, who made and end to all my*
*sin. Because the sinless Savior died,*
*my sinful soul is counted free..."*
**"Before the Throne of God Above"**
Charitie Bancroft [24]

---

[24] Bancroft, Charitie, "Before the Throne of God Above", Public Domain

Tojo (5)

## **Blessing of Repentance (5.5)**

"Setting before the soul the adultery of David, the pride of Hezekiah, the impatience of Job, the drunkenness of Noah, the blasphemy of Peter, etc., and by hiding from the soul the tears, sighs, the groans, the meltings, the humblings and repenting of these precious souls.... the Lord hath been as careful to note the saints' rising by repentance out of sin, as he hath to note their falling into sins" [25]

**Thomas Brooks**

Note the blessing of repentance found in these passages:

**Psalm 103:12** _____

**Isaiah 43:25** _____

**Isaiah 44:21-22** _____

_____

After he was confronted by Nathan for his adultery with Bathsheba and subsequent murder of Uriah, David wrote Psalm 51. He didn't make a new set of resolutions to try harder. While confessing his sin, David cried out to God:

## **"Purge me with hyssop, and I shall be clean; wash me, and I shall be whiter than snow."**

Look back at the quote from Brooks and note that Scripture never painted a picture of perfection in the heroes of the faith. God revealed both their sins and their repentance. We are called to follow the same path when we stumble.

---

[25] Brooks, Thomas, *Precious Remedies against Satan's Devices* Carlisle, Pa. The Banner of Truth Trust, 1652

| Axis Powers

## **Special Orders (5.6)**

Spiritual warfare is as much a part of Christian life as covered dish suppers and mission trips. As Believers we can count on the fact that Satan will attack. Our response to him will influence the impact that will have on our lives.

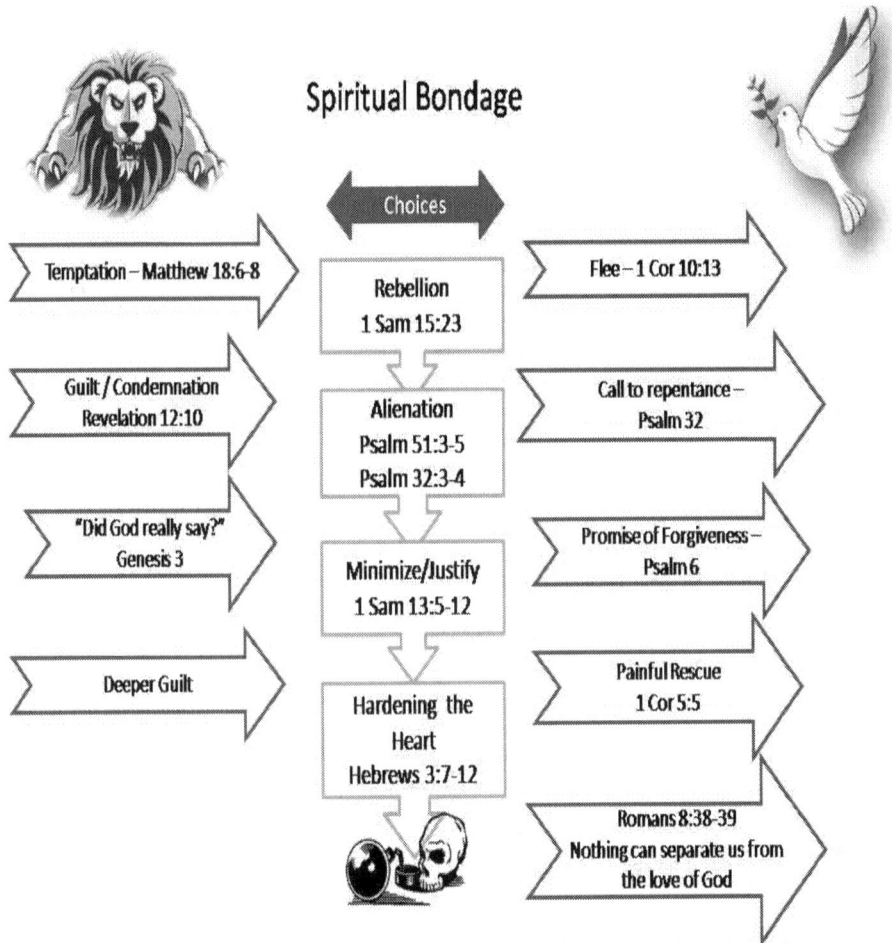

### Spiritual Bondage

**Choices**

- Temptation – Matthew 18:6-8 → Rebellion (1 Sam 15:23) → Flee – 1 Cor 10:13
- Guilt / Condemnation Revelation 12:10 → Alienation (Psalm 51:3-5, Psalm 32:3-4) → Call to repentance – Psalm 32
- "Did God really say?" Genesis 3 → Minimize/Justify (1 Sam 13:5-12) → Promise of Forgiveness – Psalm 6
- Deeper Guilt → Hardening the Heart (Hebrews 3:7-12) → Painful Rescue 1 Cor 5:5
- Romans 8:38-39 Nothing can separate us from the love of God

*If we confess our sins, he is faithful and just to forgive us our sins and to cleanse us from all unrighteousness*

## Tojo (5)

Israel's first king was Saul. He was a man who exhibited humility at the first but whose character was not strong enough to handle his own personal exaltation. Matthew 18:6-8 serves as our warning to do whatever it takes to defeat the temptation. But Saul failed to heed that warning. 1 Corinthians 10:13 reminds us that God has already provided a way out... flee!

In 1 Samuel 15:23 we learn that Saul resisted the counsel of Samuel and took matters into his own hands. The downward spiral from temptation to spiritual bondage comes with a series of choices. When tempted we can flee or we can fall. Saul took the next step toward Spiritual bondage.

When Satan condemns us, God calls us to repent. As we devolve more deeply in this cycle, it becomes more difficult to break the cycle – yet God is there at every step, inviting repentance and release from Satan's prison camp. Revelation 12:30 reminds us that Satan is the accuser. Even at this point in the cycle... after we have sinned, God offers the blessing of repentance and restoration in Psalm 32 and Psalm 51.

Rejecting the offer of repentance, Satan arrives on the scene to challenge God's authority: "Did God really say?". So we justify and minimize our actions as we move toward the hardening of our hearts. The antidote is found in **Psalm 6:8-9**:

> "The Lord has heard the sound of my weeping.
> The Lord has heard my plea;
> The Lord accepts my prayer"

Even when we harden our hearts, God will use disciplinary means (1 Corinthians 5:5) to call true Believers back to himself. There is no point in the cycle where God does not offer a way out. No matter how far we run from God, he will pursue. In that pursuit, He may find it necessary to discipline us in order to our eyes back to Him.

| Axis Powers

Like a parasite, Satan uses temptation to draw us into sin. Once he gets us there, he becomes the tyrant, holding us in chains as long as he possibly can by keeping our eyes focused on our guilt and off of the promises of Christ.

All of us will sin and fall short of God's glory. Whether or not a particular sin leads us into bondage depends on our response. We can grieve, resist, or quench the Holy Spirit, but He will never leave us.

Each step of the way, the chains grow stronger – but the path to freedom is always there for the true Believer. Ultimately, we find our peace in the promise of God – in whom we are sealed for eternity. He is the one who began his work in you and He will be faithful to carry it to the end. For the Believer, the bondage of sin brings pain – but the chains of bondage will be broken by Christ, himself.

> "[38] For I am sure that neither death nor life, nor angels nor rulers, nor things present nor things to come, nor powers, [39] nor height nor depth, nor anything else in all creation, will be able to separate us from the love of God in Christ Jesus our Lord."
>
> **Romans 8:38-39**

Schutzstaffel (6)

# Schutzstaffel (6)

Hitler's Schutzstaffel, or "S.S." was an elite group of men who were organized in 1925. Membership in the S.S. was restricted to those who were pure Aryan Germans. The name "Schutzstaffel" is translated "Protective Echelon". In its early years the S.S. had a primary role of protecting Adolf Hitler. Over time, this elite group of men expanded in terms of membership and in power.

Members of the S.S. had to prove their Aryan purity. They were not allowed to have any Jewish blood in their lineage. They were considered the elite of the elite in their racial superiority and in their role in the Nazi leadership.

Members of the S.S. had sworn eternal loyalty to Adolf Hitler and became a group of men who were often seen as the personification of evil. While they were often men of fine social standing who seemed quite normal, they were, in truth, ruthless, violent, powerful men who seemed to be devoid of any ounce of empathy when carrying out their duties.

Warrior 63

| Axis Powers

## S.A. (Sturmabteilung)
Literally translated "Storm Detachment", the S.A. also known as "Brownshirts" served an important role in Adolf Hitler's rise to power. The Brownshirts were known for their violence and intimidation of anyone who disagreed with the Nazi cause.

The S.A. provided protection during Nazi party rallies and for Adolf Hitler himself. Additionally, they were active in disrupting the activities of the Nazi political opponents. Their tactics extended to include trade unions and Jewish businesses.

The Schutzstaffel (Hitler's S.S.) was originally formed as a branch of the S.A. Over time, the S.S. separated from the Brownshirts and became the dominant force within the Nazi party.

## Night of the Long Knives
Between 30 June and 2 July 1934, at the encouragement of Heinrich Himmler and Hermann Göring, Hitler carried out a series of executions that included some of the leaders of the S.A. including its leader, Ernst Röhm.

The "Night of the Long Knives" was carried out to eliminate any challenges to Hitler's authority and consolidate his power in Nazi Germany. The official death toll for the purge was 85, although unofficial estimates were much higher.

Because of their tactics, the Brownshirts had become unpopular with the German people so Hitler used the purge to enhance his own reputation. Even though the killings were outside of German law, the German courts gave their support to Hitler. Their actions (or lack thereof) effectively made him the "supreme administrator of justice" of the German people.

The S.S. was formed in 1925 with only eight (8) members who had pledged their loyalty to Adolf Hitler. Hitler's consolidation of power and the Schutzstaffel's dominant role in his administration were both cemented on the "Night of Long Knives". Their power, authority, and impact would only grow from this point forward.

# Schutzstaffel (6)

Under the leadership of Heinrich Himmler, the S.S. grew to more than 800,000 members by the end of the war. Under his leadership, the Schutzstaffel functioned under several different groups, each with a distinct purpose within the overall mission of terror, intimidation, and murder.

## S.S. Reichsführer Heinrich Himmler

The position of "Reichsführer" was the most powerful position in Hitler's S.S. Heinrich Himmler held that position from 1929 to 1945. He was head of the entire Nazi police force including the S.D. and the Gestapo. Himmler was Minister of the Interior and commander of the Waffen S.S. and the Home Army. One of Hitler's most sinister henchmen, he was also in charge of the death camps in the East. The account of Himmler's life and his impact on the rise and fall of the Nazi state make a gripping and horrifying story.

Although Adolf Hitler held the ultimate responsibility for the Holocaust, it was Heinrich Himmler who essentially laid the plans and devised the schemes that led to the killings of six million Jews.

## What about Gestapo?

Geheime Staatspolizei, better known as "Gestapo" functioned as the German secret police force. Although their powers and activities frequently overlapped, the Gestapo had a separate and distinct identity and function from the S.S. The Gestapo worked through a network of informants to identify and arrest enemies of the State.

With the power of arrest and imprisonment without due process, the Gestapo used the Peoples Court to prosecute political enemies. Punishment often included the death penalty.

By way of contrast, the Schutzstaffel (S.S.) was military in its origin, but also carried with it the powers of arrest, prosecution, and punishment. Under Hitler, both agencies were united under the leadership of Heinrich Himmler.

| Axis Powers

### Sicherheltsdienst (SD)
The "S.D." was an elite security detail responsible for protecting Hitler and other senior Nazi officials. The S.D. was led by Reinhard Heydrich from 1931 to 1945.

### Concentration Camps
The S.S. did not create the first concentration camps in Germany. Most had been created by civilian authorities and other agencies for the purpose of incarcerating political enemies of the Nazi regime.

From 1933 to 1934, Hitler called on Himmler to organize a centralized concentration camp system using the camp at Dachau as a model for other camps to follow with the S.S. in control. By the end of 1934, all of the concentration camps were under the command of S.S. officers who ruled with unlimited authority.

Over time, the concentration camp system expanded and took center-stage in what we now call the Holocaust, where unimaginable brutality, murder, torture and other horror stories were the result.

### Operation Tannenberg
Prior to the September 1939 invasion of Poland, the Gestapo had compiled a list of 61,000 Polish citizens who were targeted for imprisonment or execution. In the immediate aftermath of the invasion that started World War II, Operation Tannenberg was launched.

The S.S. formed "Einsatzgruppen" (mobile killing squads) under the leadership of Reinhard Heydrich for the purpose of executing targeted groups of people considered a threat to the Nazi cause.

The initial phase of Operation Tannenberg resulted in 760 mass executions resulting in more that 20,000 deaths at the hands of these killing squads. The dead included Polish "elites", Polish Jews, and Catholic clergy, among others.

## Schutzstaffel (6)

Following those actions, members of the S.S. executed patients in several hospitals in Poland. Some patients were shot. Others were killed in mobile gas chambers.

The executions continued into 1940 and expanded to surrounding areas. The final death toll from Operation Tannenberg and subsequent operations is estimated to be in excess of 100,000.

Operation Tannenberg became the standard for the mass executions carried out later by the S.S. throughout the war.

### Operation Reinhard [26]

Adolf Hitler and Hermann Göring gave Reinhard Heydrich the responsibility of drafting plans for a solution to what was known as the "Jewish Question". Heydrich had already gained a reputation for his ruthless cruelty.

The man Hitler called "the man with an iron heart" had helped organize the coordinated attacks on Jewish homes and businesses during the "Night of Broken Glass" (Kristallnacht). He was directly responsible for the organization and activities of the task force Einsatzgruppen which carried out the murders of more than 2 million civilians throughout the Reich.

On 27 May 1942, Heydrich has critically wounded by a team of Czech and Slovak agents. He died a week later. S.S. repercussions from the assassination included the utter destruction of two villages and the mass murder of all men and boys over 16 years old. Most of the women and children were taken to Nazi concentration camps.

As a result of his service to Hitler, the plan to exterminate Polish Jews from October 1941 to November 1943 was code-named "Operation Reinhard". Under the plan, a number of concentration

---

[26] United States Holocaust Museum, encyclopedia.ushmm.org, "Operation Reinhard (Einsatz Reinhard), accessed 25 February 2019

## Axis Powers

camps became extermination camps. The goals of Operation Reinhard, as articulated by S.S. General Odilo Globocnik were:

- Exploit the skilled labor of Polish Jews before killing them;
- Secure/Confiscate personal property of the Jews (clothing, currency, jewelry, etc.);
- Identify and secure immovable assets (businesses, factories, real estate);
- And to "resettle" (kill) the Polish Jews

The overwhelming majority of the victims were deported from Polish ghettos. S.S. forces liquidated the ghettos and brought the Jews to extermination centers by rail. The estimated death toll from Operation Reinhard was 1.7 million Jews in addition to an unknown number of Roma, Poles and Soviet prisoners of war.

**Schutzstaffel**
Some of history's most notorious names came in a Nazi S.S. uniform with the memorable "S.S." rune on their uniforms. They were Hitler's voice of enforcement throughout the Third Reich. They acted with impunity. They acted without restriction or restraint. They acted outside any formal system of justice.

There are thousands of stories emanating from the S.S. and the Holocaust detailing a level of brutality beyond comprehension. Women were tortured and babies had their skulls crushed for the crime of crying. Some brutality seemed to be carried out for the pure pleasure and entertainment of the S.S. member carrying it out.

More than 70 years after the war, history continues to remember the names of men like Heinrich Himmler, Reinhard Heydrich, Hermann Göring, Joseph Goebbels, Josef Mengele, Adolf Eichmann, Rudolf Hoess and more.

Schutzstaffel (6)

## **Abaddon - Destroyer (6.1)**

Satan's defeat and ultimate sentence was proclaimed in the Garden of Eden. His defeat was sealed at the Cross of Christ. But his final judgement is yet to be carried out when Christ himself will cast him and his followers into an eternal bottomless pit.

Until then, and throughout history, he has proven himself to be a powerful and formidable enemy to followers of Christ. He is called "Apollyon (Greek) or Abaddon (Hebrew)", meaning "destroyer" in Revelation 9:1.

He appears as a serpent in Genesis, a "roaring lion" in 1 Peter 5, and as a dragon in the book of Revelation. In Ephesians 6, we are called to put on our spiritual armor to "extinguish flaming darts of the evil one". The images reveal an intense physical battle that is fought in the spiritual realm.

Many understate Satan's power by characterizing him as a defeated enemy whose weapons are limited to "whispering temptations and accusations" at the Believer. If you have ever watched the National Geographic Channel (or in the old days *"Mutual of Omaha's Wild Kingdom"*) - that's really not an accurate picture of the way a lion works.

Scripture describes Satan as a "lion" and uses the term devour and we need to understand why, lest we underestimate the capabilities of our mortal enemy.

In real life, the lion waits for the unsuspecting victim, usually the weakest animal in the herd, to wander away from the herd - becoming easy prey. When the lion attacks, bones are crushed and flesh is torn. That is the image of Satan as portrayed in Scripture.

| Axis Powers

# Symphony of Terror (6.2)

As Believers we face three (3) enemies, not one. But we must not make the mistake of seeing them as three separate threats. Demonic beings, the world culture, and our own flesh are willing participants in an orchestra directed by Satan himself.

Daniel served under a number of pagan kings, including Cyrus (king of Persia). Describe the scene that Daniel was experiencing in **Daniel 10:1-3**:

_____

_____

_____

Notice the physical effects on Daniel and those around him: **Daniel 10:7-9**

_____

_____

How does Scripture describe what was happening during Daniel's three (3) week fast? **Daniel 10:10-14**:

_____

_____

_____

Describe Daniel's physical countenance in **verses 15-17**:

_____

_____

_____

Daniel was appointed to receive a vision from the Lord. As he is engaged in spiritual warfare through fasting and prayer, there is a real battle being waged on his behalf with Satan and his demons.

Warrior – Page 70

## Schutzstaffel (6)

What encouragement does God provide through this messenger in **Daniel 10:18-21?**

_____

_____

_____


What is your "default" view of Satan? Do you tend to minimize him as a metaphor for evil? Do you tend toward the other end of the spectrum – seeing his hand in every trial in your life?

_____

_____

_____


We should not make the mistake of believing that every dream or "vision" is a message from God nor that every physical trial is demonic. We do need to be on the alert for the "roaring lion" of 1 Peter 5:8-9. While we are involved in doing Christ's work, the enemy will respond. There will be a real battle, both here and in the spiritual realm.

> **"Not everything occurs because of demonic schemes. But everything can be exploited by demonic forces**...The fact is, you are going to be assailed... Your first responsibility is to be aware of the battle, your second responsibility is to depend on God's strength and your third responsibility is to use the protection God has provided"
>
> Chip Ingram [27]

---

[27] Ingram, Chip, *The Invisible War*, Baker Books, Grand Rapids, Michigan, 2006

| Axis Powers

## **Power to Persecute (6.3)**

"Satan and his forces have a plan to terrorize your soul, to render you impotent as a believer, to make you worthless to the cause of Christ, and to make your life one of misery and spiritual defeat" **- Chip Ingram** [28]

From the following verses, how many ways are Satan's powers on display?

**Job 1:12-22**

**Job 2:4-10**

It would be a mistake to credit Satan with every malady that we encounter. Sickness, death, pain, and hardship are some of the consequences of the fall. In John 16:33, Jesus tells us that "in this world you will have tribulation".

However, Scripture does not minimize Satan's power on earth. The Bible is filled with examples of demonic activity that has the power to inflict physical pain and death, to incite persecution and to inflict emotional and psychological damage, even using the forces of nature itself.

This was what Job experienced. However, Satan could not attack Job unless God allowed it. Satan's power is always limited by God's hand. Repeat that: Satan's power is ALWAYS limited by God's hand.

---

[28] Ingram, Chip, *The Invisible War*, Baker Books, Grand Rapids, Michigan, 2006

Schutzstaffel (6)

## **Special Orders (6.4)**

There are Christians who truly believe that Satan is an impotent, defeated enemy who is relegated to whispering temptations into the ears of Believers. Indeed, Satan is defeated. But he is by no means impotent.

In the case of Job, the Chaldeans and Sabeans were not able to attack until God allowed Satan to incite them. In the case of Saul, he was tormented by an evil spirit and then proceeded to attack David at every opportunity.

Were Hitler's S.S. carrying out their evil under direct orders from Satan? Were the terrorists under the influence of Satan when they flew the planes into the World Trade Center buildings on September 11? What about the killing fields of Cambodia or the people murdered by Idi Amin? Satan's direct involvement (if any) in any or all of these events is unknowable without direct revelation from God. What we do know is that Abaddon – the destroyer, is real. He the powerful lion of 1 Peter 5 and he has the capacity of inflicting serious pain.

We often find ourselves wondering – "Is this present conflict/trial the result of a frontal attack by Satan or not?" In view of God's conversation with Satan in Job – does it matter?

> "And though this world with devils filled
> Should threaten to undo us
> We will not fear, for God hath willed
> His truth to triumph through us.
> The prince of darkness grim
> We tremble not for him,
> His rage we can endure
> For low his doom is sure.
> One little word will fell him."
> **"A Mighty Fortress"** [29]

---

[29] Luther, Martin, "A Mighty Fortress", c 1529

## Axis Powers

The past three chapters have been devoted to understanding Satan (the Adversary). Many Believers grant intellectual assent to his existence, but live as if he does not exist. Others see him as almost equal to God himself.

It bears repeating the words of C.S. Lewis:
> "There are two equal and opposite errors into which our race can fall about the devils. One is to disbelieve in their existence. **The other is to believe and to feel an excessive and unhealthy interest in them**" [30]

- Satan is powerful – but God is Omnipotent
- Satan is crafty – but God is Omniscient
- Satan is fast – but God is Omnipresent

The Book of Job demonstrates the power of Satan when he is unleashed, but chapter 1 makes it abundantly clear that God holds the end of that leash.

> "And the Lord said to Satan, 'Have you considered my servant Job, that there is none like him on the earth, a blameless and upright man, who fears God and turns away from evil?' Then Satan answered the Lord and said, 'Does Job fear God for no reason? Have you not put a hedge around him and his house and all that he has, on every side? You have blessed the work of his hands, and his possessions have increased in the land.'"
>
> **Job 1:8-10**

**The Believer's role:**
Christians are not called to defeat Satan. Christ has already done that. Our role is to glorify God and to win others away from Satan by being the salt and light of a dying world. As the battles rage, Satan and his demonic forces will attack, and he will use the world and our flesh against us. Our call is to stand firm in the battle and to be on the alert for his devices.

---

[30] Lewis, C.S. – *The Screwtape Letters*, C.S. Lewis Pte. Ltd. 1942

## Schutzstaffel (6)

After the September 11th attacks (2001) John Piper [31] wrote:

> "... our vision of God in relation to evil and suffering was shown to be frivolous. **The church has not been spending its energy to go deep with the unfathomable God of the Bible**. Against the overwhelming weight and seriousness of the Bible, much of the church is choosing, at this very moment, to become more light and shallow and entertainment-oriented, and therefore successful in its irrelevance to massive suffering and evil. The popular God of fun-church is simply too small and too affable to hold a hurricane in his hand. The biblical categories of God's sovereignty lie like landmines in the pages of the Bible waiting for someone to seriously open the book. They don't kill, but they do explode trivial notions of the Almighty."

All true Believers are engaged in a battle with the world, the flesh and the devil. That battle is frequently quite painful. The enemy is powerful and often very effective in inflicting damage.

Those who teach Christianity as a means to a prosperous, healthy, and pain-free life are heretics in the worst way. Spiritual warfare, trials, and adversity are integral to living out our lives as disciples of Christ.

We should not be surprised when the fiery trials come our way. Neither should we give the enemy more credit than he deserves. God is sovereign. Satan is no match.

Repeating Martin Luther

> "And though this world with devils filled
> Should threaten to undo us
> We will not fear, for God hath willed
> His truth to triumph through us"

---

[31] John Piper and Justin Taylor, *Suffering and the Sovereignty of God*, 2006, Crossway Books, Wheaton, Illinois,

| Axis Powers

# Peace for our Time (7)

## 30 September 1938

Lord Neville Chamberlain took over as Prime Minister of Great Britain in 1937. It was his belief that appeasement of Hitler in the "annexing" of Austria and part of Czechoslovakia was preferable over challenging the Nazis and plunging Europe into another war.

"We, the German Fuhrer and Chancellor, and the British Prime Minister, have had a further meeting today and are agreed in recognizing that the question of Anglo-German relations is of the first importance for our two countries and for Europe.

"We regard the agreement signed last night and the Anglo-German Naval Agreement as symbolic of the desire of our two peoples never to go to war with one another again. We are resolved that the method of consultation shall be the method adopted to deal with any other questions that may concern our two countries, and we are determined to continue our efforts to remove possible sources of difference, and thus to contribute to assure the peace of Europe.

Neville Chamberlain

## Peace for our Time (7)

"My good friends, for the second time
in our history, a British Prime Minister has returned from
Germany bringing peace with honour.
I believe it is peace for our time...
Go home and get a nice quiet sleep."

### Pierre Laval

He was named Time Magazine's "Man of the Year" in January, 1932, became Prime Minister of France in 1935 and worked toward appeasement as the solution to Benito Mussolini's aggression into Abyssinia (present day Ethiopia) Laval's attitude toward Hitler was more than one of appeasement, his was outright collaboration with Hitler.

Laval was named Prime Minister of Vichy, France. Among other actions he is noted for:
- Banning the slogan "Liberty, Equality, Fraternity";
- Working with Nazis to integrate France into the new order;
- Sending French Jews to Germany for incarceration;
- Sending French workers to Germany as slaves;
- Working with Marshal Petain to "protect the French people from suffering"

### Laval's speech to the French people
6 June 1944 (D-Day)

"You are not in the war. You must not take part in the fighting. If you do not observe this rule, if you show proof of indiscipline, you will provoke reprisals the harshness of which the government would be powerless to moderate. You would suffer both physically and materially, and you would add to your country's misfortunes. You will refuse to heed the insidious appeals, which will be addressed to you. Those who ask you to stop work or invite you to revolt are the enemies of our country. You will refuse to aggravate the foreign war on our soil with the horror of civil war.... At this moment fraught with drama, when the war has been carried on to our territory, show by your worthy and disciplined attitude that you are thinking of France and only of her."

| Axis Powers

**6 October 1945** – Convicted of treason, Pierre Laval swallowed cyanide in a suicide attempt. A physician saved his life and he was executed two weeks later.

**Winston Churchill**
Where Laval, Chamberlain, and many others pursued peace with Adolf Hitler through appeasement and compromise. Churchill had a starkly different attitude. He believed that appeasing Hitler would only whet his appetite for more power, leading the world down a dangerous path. He is often quoted as saying "An appeaser is one who feeds a crocodile – hoping it will eat him last."

"Each one hopes that if he feeds the crocodile enough, the crocodile will eat him last. All of them hope that the storm will pass before their turn comes to be devoured"
**Winston Churchill**

*Time Magazine*
1940 January 29, Time, Volume 35 Issue 5, Invitation to War, Page 27, Time Inc., New York.

**13 May 1940: Winston Churchill:**
"You ask, what is our policy? I can say: It is to wage war, by sea, land and air, with all our might and with all the strength that God can give us; to wage war against a monstrous tyranny, never surpassed in the dark, lamentable catalogue of human crime. That is our policy.

"You ask, what is our aim? I can answer in one word: It is victory, victory at all costs, victory in spite of all terror, victory, however long and hard the road may be; for without victory, there is no survival."

## Peace for our Time (7)

Churchill referred to Hitler's Nazi Germany as a "monstrous tyranny".

**Peace for our time?**

Throughout human history there have been wars that were fought where negotiation and compromise would have been proven the better choice. Neville Chamberlain believed that Hitler would eventually become satisfied and the aggression would stop at the British border. Laval went even further, attempting to hang on to his French heritage with an unholy alliance with the enemy.

The choice is not always clear. In the end, and to his credit, it was Neville Chamberlain's voice over the radio that announced Britain's decision to war against Nazi Germany. His speech on 3 September 1939 reads, in part:[32]

> "This morning the British Ambassador in Berlin handed the German Government a final Note stating that, unless we heard from them by 11 o'clock that they were prepared at once to withdraw their troops from Poland, a state of war would exist between us.
>
> "I have to tell you now that no such undertaking has been received, and that consequently this country is at war with Germany."

Note Chamberlain's choice of words in closing his speech:

> "Now may God bless you all. May He defend the right. It is the evil things that we shall be fighting against - brute force, bad faith, injustice, oppression and persecution - and against them I am certain that the right will prevail."

Prime Minister Chamberlain was not successful in his efforts to achieve peace through appeasement, but he took a strong stand when he realized the evil that he was facing.

---

[32] BBC Archive, 1939 Transcript of Neville Chamberlain's Declaration of War, BBC.co.uk

Axis Powers

## **Friendship with the World (7.1)**

"Our calling is not only to order your own lives by divine principles but also to engage the world...The culture war is not just about abortion, homosexual rights, or the decline of public education. These are only the skirmishes. The real war is a cosmic struggle between worldviews – between the Christian worldview and various secular and spiritual worldviews arrayed against it" –
**Charles Colson** [33]

Friendship with the world can look and sound very attractive. Appeasement, cooperation and even collaboration can be tempting. What the world offers stimulates our senses with images of power, wealth, material possessions, unrestrained sexual gratification, glitter, sparkle and "respect" and adoration of other men.

Listen to the voice of the World in Laval's speech. "You are not in the war. You must not take part in the fighting".

The world invites you into a life where everyone accepts everyone else... but only on their terms.

How does Scripture describe the "world"?

**John 3:16** _____

**James 4:1-4** _____

Some will read John 3:16 and interpret it as saying God loves the world so much he would never condemn anyone to Hell. In reality, God so loved the world that he was willing to put his Son on the Cross to provide a way to escape this culture and its consequences.

---

[33] Colson, Charles, *How Now Shall We Live*, Tyndale House Publishers, 1999

Peace for our Time (7)

## **Tolerance? (7.2)**

The world extols "tolerance" as the single greatest virtue, but the word "tolerance" literally means to put up with something we don't really like, such as when a person has a high tolerance for pain. **Christians are not called to "tolerate", we are called to love**.

The challenge is to live "in the world" but not be conformed to its value system. Instead of allowing the world to change us, we are called to rescue people from their condition. The challenge to every Christian is to be the salt and light in a world that tolerates everything but the Truth, and still demonstrate the love of Christ that transcends the world's definition of "tolerance"

How should the we, as Believers view the world culture?

**Titus 2:11-14** _____

_____

_____

**Romans 8:18-23** _____

_____

_____

Notice the use of the phrase "bondage of corruption". A devolving world is a dying world that is imprisoned by sin, death, and Satan. Tolerance is not an act of "love". Tolerance is standing on the outside of a prison cell and watching others die there. **Love demands a rescue mission**.

In Judges 6 were are told that God called Gideon to lead his people out of captivity, but his first call was to tear down idols that Israel had constructed. Gideon was not called to tolerate the social "norms" of his own people. He was called to tear them down in order to lead his people out of captivity.

| Axis Powers

## The Influence Continuum (7.3)

In his book, *The Disciplines of Grace* [34], Jerry Bridges speaks of what he calls the "influence continuum", using Psalm 1:1-3 as a platform for the illustration.

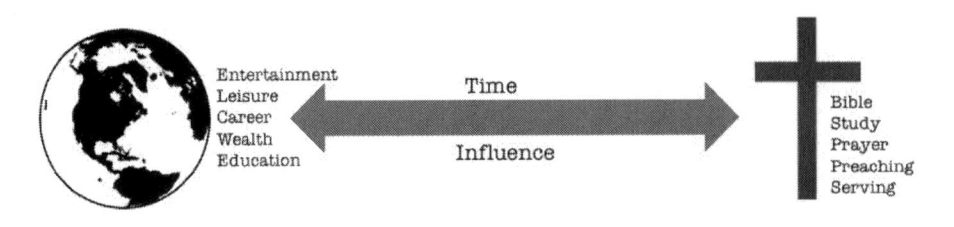

```
                Entertainment
                Leisure            Time                        Bible
                Career    <--------------->                    Study
                Wealth             Influence                   Prayer
                Education                                      Preaching
                                                               Serving
```

**Psalm 1** – What are the warnings and what is our calling as it relates to the world?

All true Believers live somewhere on that continuum and we are likely to move back and forth along the line throughout our life. We are influenced by the world – that is an inescapable fact. How much we are influenced by God is an act of volition.

**As Bridges says**:
"What determines whether we are moving to the left or the right? The psalmist gives us the answer: our attitude toward the Word of God and the time we spend thinking about it"

In Genesis 14 and 19, we read about Abraham's nephew Lot. Lot was attracted to the city of Sodom and wanted to live as close to the city as possible without being contaminated by its sin. In the end, he stooped to the level of offering his daughters to the lusting mob outside his own doors.

---

[34] Bridges, Jerry, *The Disciplines of Grace*, 1994, NaviPress Publishing, Colorado Springs, Co

Peace for our Time (7)

## **Hunger for God (7.4)**

"The greatest enemy of hunger for God is not poison but apple pie. It is not the banquet of the wicked that dulls our appetite for heaven, but endless nibbling at the table of the world. It is not the X-rated video, but the prime-time dribble of triviality we drink in every night." **John Piper** [35]

**Romans 12:1-2**     What is the call?

_____

_____

_____

**Romans 12:3-21**     Is there anything in this passage that stands out as counter-cultural?

_____

_____

_____

"Do not love the world or the things in the world. If anyone loves the world, the love of the Father is not in him. [16] For all that is in the world—the desires of the flesh and the desires of the eyes and pride of life—is not from the Father but is from the world. [17] And the world is passing away along with its desires, but whoever does the will of God abides forever."
**1 John 2:15-17**

Satan's world culture can be attractive. Culture demands that we remove our "religion" from the workplace or the political arena. Culture demands that we accept (even celebrate) every form of human behavior without exception or limitation. Scripture makes it clear that we are not called to get comfortable with this world. We have a purpose here – but conformity is not it.

---

[35] Piper, John, *Hunger for God*, Crossway 1997

Axis Powers

## **Foreign Prison (7.5)**

We are called to live as aliens in a world that is under the dominion of by Satan. We do damage to his cause when we win others to Christ. We do damage to his cause when we live our lives in a manner that pleases Christ. We do damage to his cause when we influence our cultures by exercising our call to be the "salt and the light of the world".

> According to **John 15:18-21**, how should we expect the world to respond to us as Believers?
> _____
> _____
> _____
> _____
> _____

Darkness and light cannot coexist. Light always dispels darkness. Likewise, when you add salt to meat, a chemical reaction takes place that slows down the process of decay. The world's culture is decaying in darkness.

Imagine going into a prisoner of war camp to rescue its prisoners. When you get there you find good food, comfortable accommodations so you decide to stay awhile. The outward appearance of the world can be enticing. If we get comfortable with Satan's culture, they will accept us as fellow prisoners in their death camp.

We are called to win others to Christ through our winsome and gracious presentation of the Gospel. We are not called to make them comfortable in a world governed by Satan.

Peace for our Time (7)

## **Special Orders (7.6)**

When Neville Chamberlain went to Munich, he negotiated with the enemy with the best intentions. He sincerely believed that war could be avoided if the world made the concessions demanded by Hitler. At the time, those concessions were not viewed as major concessions.

But when Chamberlain finally recognized Adolf Hitler as an evil force to be dealt with, he declared war. Evil knows no compromise and will meet every concession with a demand for more. Hitler was Churchill's hungry crocodile. His appetite was insatiable.

According to Pew Research[36] statistics, American's who identify themselves as "Christians" have declined from 78.4% to 70.6% from 2007 to 2014, while those who identify as atheists, agnostics, or "nothing in particular" have increased over the same period. There are a number of factors that have probably contributed to those changes. However, in general terms, the world culture is turning away from God.

Even more alarming is that, within the numbers of Americans who identify as "Christian", we are seeing major shifts in the understanding of what defines the word "Christian" and the values that set us apart from the rest of the world. The value shift has been gradual in the past, but has accelerated in recent years due to a number of factors.

There remains a contingent of Christians who are holding fast to the foundational precepts that define true followers of Christ, but our numbers are faltering.

Many of us have seen cultural devolution that took us from the days of Lucy and Desi sleeping in twin beds to television that seems to know no limits of sexual expression.

---

[36] "America's Changing Religious Landscape", 12 May, 2015, pewforum.org

# Axis Powers

Many of us have been at the front of battles over prayer in schools, abortion, evolution vs creation, and persecution of others simply because of their skin color.

We have gone from the days of hidden magazines to rampant pornography and celebration of all types of perversions.

We have moved from conviction of sin to tolerance of sin to unrestrained celebration of all that God abhors.

Yet, behind the obvious front line battles, many professing Christians see the world and its culture as something to be embraced and even enjoyed. Many churches are avoiding the topics of sin and hell, making a casualty of the concept of "repentance".

We have seen a shift from Christ's exclusive claim to salvation to a more universalist approach to salvation in order to placate the culture's demands. Christians who defend Christ's exclusive claim to salvation are branded as "bigots", "intolerant", and even "hate groups".

Neville Chamberlain pursued peace through appeasement with Hitler and the results were devastating. Hitler took what Chamberlain offered and demanded more. His appetite was insatiable. Pure evil will never be satisfied through appeasement.

The world culture has an equally insatiable appetite for evil. Each and every concession will be met with another demand. The world loves its crocodile and wants to live in his pit.

The book of Daniel begins with the story of four (4) Hebrew adolescents who, though taken captive by the enemy, stood firm in their obedience to God. They refused to be conformed to the Babylonian lifestyle and then refused to bow before the Babylonian idols. Not only did God protect them during their obedience, but he used them as a vessel to transform the heart of King Nebuchadnezzar.

## Peace for our Time (7)

In contrast, God warned Solomon not to marry the daughters of foreign kings for they would turn his heart toward their gods. Solomon failed to heed the warning, his heart was turned and the nation of Israel suffered for hundreds of years afterward.

Being conformed to this world under the pretense of demonstrating "grace" can sound godly. However, the world (culture) is our enemy. The people captivated by it are prisoners of war. As Believers we are called to rescue them – not join them in their prison camp.

> "The kings of the earth set themselves, and the rulers take counsel together, against the Lord and against his anointed, saying, 'Let us burst their bonds apart and cast away their cords from us.' He who sits in the heavens laughs; the Lord holds them in derision"
> **Psalm 2:2-4**

Followers of Christ are no more than resident aliens, sojourners on the way to a promised eternity. We are here on a mission. The world has nothing of value to offer us, yet it needs the one thing we have to offer... the gift they want to reject. The gift of eternal life with Jesus Christ.

| Axis Powers

# Aryan Paragraph (8)

The German Evangelical Church had long considered itself a pillar in the German culture and had developed a traditional loyalty to the State.

In the 1920's, as the Nazi ideology began to gain influence, a movement emerged within the German Evangelical Church called the Deutsche Christen, or "German Christians." The "German Christians" embraced many of the nationalistic and anti-Semitic aspects of Nazi ideology. Once the Nazis came to power, this group sought the creation of a national "Reich Church" and supported distorted version of Christianity, embracing what was known as the "Aryan Paragraph".

## Aryan Paragraph (8)

Simply defined, the "Aryan Paragraph" was a clause in the statutes of any organization, or contract that reserved membership and/or rights solely to members of the "Aryan race" and specifically excluded Jews or people of Jewish descent. The Paragraph was widely instituted in social institutions throughout the Reich. More importantly, it also was gaining acceptance within the Church – both Protestant and Roman Catholic.

### "Aryan Church"

The Nazi state enacted the "Law for the Restoration of the Professional Civil Service" on 7 April 1933, calling for the dismissal or early retirement of civil servants of "non-Aryan ancestry". The objective was alienation of Jews and other "undesirable races" from society.

On 5 September 1933, the "Brown Synod" of the Evangelical Church resolved to adopt the Aryan Paragraph as church law. The Brown Synod accounted for almost half of all German Protestants at the time.

Immediately following that decision, the "Aryan Paragraph" was introduced in other churches, with some success and some opposition.

Opposition to the Aryan Paragraph first came on 14 September 1933, when 25 pastors from Nuremberg joined together to prevent its adoption, asking Bishop Hans Meister to protest the provision from his official position in the church. In their letter, they pointed out that, under the Aryan Paragraph:

> **"neither Peter nor Paul nor the Lord Christ himself would be allowed to preach in our church"**

### Church and State

In an effort to avoid conflict with German authorities, and maintain its position in the German culture, the German Church had begun adopting policies within their own churches. They had a choice – to stand for the truth and risk their very existence or to attempt to make peace with the Nazi government.

## Axis Powers

Over time, anti-Nazi sentiment grew in both Protestant and Catholic church circles, as the Nazi regime exerted greater pressure on them. In turn, the Nazi regime saw a potential for dissent in church criticism of state measures and took action to shut down any opposition to the Nazi ideology.

When a protest statement was read from the pulpits of Confessing churches in March 1935, for example, Nazi authorities reacted forcefully by briefly arresting over 700 pastors.

Over time, the majority of Germany's churches, adopted the Aryan Paragraph in one form or another in order to maintain their position in German society and avoid consequences of opposing Hitler.

### Mit Brennender Sorge [37]

On 14 March 1937, Pope Pius XI issued an Encyclical entitled "With Burning Concern" (Mit Brennender Sorge) that took issue Hitler's intrusions into the teaching of the Church. The statement addressed 43 points of concern.

While the Encyclical expressed a continuing desire to avoid conflict with the Nazi government, it also took the position that the Church would not capitulate on doctrinal truths.

In his third point, Pope Pius made statement
> "We wished to spare the Faithful of Germany...the trials and difficulties they would have had to face, given the circumstances..."

In is seventh point, the Pope takes direct aim at Hitler himself. He speaks of someone who teaches "pantheistic confusion" and who diminishes the attributes of God.

---

[37] "Mit Brennender Sorge", w2.vatican.va, Pius XI Encyclicals, Copyright – Libreria Editrice Vaticana

## Aryan Paragraph (8)

In his eighth point, Pope Pius took issue with anyone who would exalt race or state to an "idolatrous level" and described him as one who "distorts and perverts" the order of the world planned and created by God.

The Encyclical, which was being read from Catholic pulpits around Germany, was confiscated by the Gestapo

### The "Confessing Church" (Bekennende Kirche)

Three factions developed in the German protestant church. There were those who pushed for a "Nazified" church, complicit with Nazi racial ideology; those who vehemently opposed that ideology; and "neutral" church leaders who sought to resolve the schism in the church and still avoid reprisals from the Nazi leadership.

The "Aryan Paragraph" became the voice of Nazi ideology in the Evangelical Church, giving it protection against persecution from the Nazi government. As a separate race, non-Aryans (Jews) were not permitted to become members of the church – even through Baptism.

The "Confessing Church" emerged as the opposition to the German Church. The most famous members of the which were the theologian Dietrich Bonhoeffer, who was eventually executed for his role in the conspiracy to overthrow the regime, and Pastor Martin Niemöller, who spent seven years in concentration camps for his criticisms of Hitler.

**Dietrich Bonhoeffer** bitterly opposed the "Aryan Paragraph" and was instrumental in organizing the anti-Nazi Confessing Church in Barmen, Germany. Bonhoeffer argued that the Aryan Paragraph sacrificed Christian precepts to political ideology. If "non-Aryans" were banned from the ministry, he argued, then their colleagues should resign in solidarity, even if this meant the establishment of a new church that would remain free of Nazi influence.

Bonhoeffer fought against the organized church in Germany that wanted to make peace with the Nazi leadership – ignoring the evil that had overtaken their country and their church.

# Axis Powers

**Martin Niemoller** was the central leader in the creation of the "Confessing Church". He, along with Karl Barth and Dietrich Bonhoeffer composed the Barmen declaration that set the church in opposition to the "Nazified" version of the German church.

The Nazi state saw the Confessing Church as a threat and the conflict continued throughout the Holocaust and World War II, with many in its leadership being persecuted.

Niemoller was tried for treason in 1932 – but was only given a "light" sentence. In response, Hitler had him imprisoned as a "personal prisoner" of the State and Niemoller remained in various concentration camps for the duration of the war.

### Peace at all costs

"The general tactic by the leadership of both Protestant and Catholic churches in Germany was caution with respect to protest and compromise with the Nazi state leadership wherever possible. There was criticism within both churches concerning Nazi racialized ideology and notions of 'Aryanism'. As a consequence, movements emerged in both churches to defend church members who were considered "non-Aryan" under Nazi racial laws (e.g., Jews who had converted). Yet throughout this period there was virtually no public opposition to antisemitism or any readiness by church leaders to publicly oppose the regime on the issues of antisemitism and state-sanctioned violence against the Jews." [38]

The German church had gotten so comfortable in its role within the German culture that it was ill-prepared for the hostile invasion of the Nazi ideology. The Church is not called to conform for the purposes of "peace". We are called to change the world. We are called to the battlefield.

---

[38] United States Holocaust Memorial Museum, Usshmm.org

Aryan Paragraph (8)

## **Playground or Battlefield (8.1)**

"In the early days, when Christianity exercised a dominant influence over American thinking, men conceived the world to be a battleground. Our fathers believed in sin and the devil and hell as constituting one force, and they believed in God and righteousness and heaven as the other. By their very nature, these forces were opposed to each other forever in deep, grave, irreconcilable hostility.

"How different today. The fact remains the same, but the interpretation has changed completely. Men think of the world not as a battleground, but as a playground. We are not here to fight; we are here to frolic".

**A.W. Tozer** [39]

**Matthew 5:13-14** – Consider the call to be salt and light. How does this call correlate with our approach to this world?

_____

_____

_____

_____

Tozer's comments are convicting. When Believers see the world as a playground, we seek to enjoy its "benefits", disregard its risks, and moral deterioration and our perspective shifts away from our eternal calling.

Light always dispels darkness. When salt is applied to meat, it retards the rotting process. When we, as Christians, decide to adopt the world's value system, we become part of the darkness and part of the decaying process.

---

[39] Tozer, A.W. – *This World: Playground or Battleground*, Christian Publications, 1989

| Axis Powers

## **Truth (8.2)**

"The world proclaims self-esteem and the church is glutted with books on how to accept and love yourself (even when your life is filled with sin). The world extols tolerance as the chief virtue, and the church is quick to tolerate every form of perversion under the banner of grace"

**Steven Cole.** [40]

Consider the passages below as they relate to churches who seek to please its followers:

**Romans 16:17-18**  _____
**1 Thessalonians 2:3-6**  _____
_____
_____
_____
_____

"You know, I'm very careful about saying who would and wouldn't go to heaven. I don't know ...from the Christian faith this is what I believe. But I just think that only God with judge a person's heart. I spent a lot of time in India with my father. I don't know all about their religion. But I know they love God. And I don't know. I've seen their sincerity" [41]

**Joel Osteen**

Pastor Osteen's sentiments can be found in many forms and in many churches across the country, as the professing church attempts to please the its followers with messages of comfort and prosperity.

---

[40] Cole, Steven J, *How Temptation Works*, Genesis 3:1-7, January 14, 1996

[41] CNN Larry King Live, "Interview with Joel Osteen, 20 June 2005, Transcript from CNN.com

## Aryan Paragraph (8)

But the message is like giving a sugar-pill to a dying cancer patient whose real need is surgery or radiation to treat the disease.

> "The preachers of the gospel have also their courtesy and their pleasing manner, but joined with honesty, so that they neither soothe men with vain praises, nor flatter their vices: but impostors allure men by flattery, and spare and indulge their vices, that they may keep them attached to themselves."[42]
>
> **John Calvin**

**According to Randy Alcorn:** [43]

> "Truth without grace breeds a self-righteous legalism that poisons the church and pushes the world away from Christ. Grace without truth breeds moral indifference and keeps people from seeing their need for Christ.
>
> "Attempts to 'soften' the gospel by minimizing truth keep people from Jesus. Attempts to 'toughen' the gospel by minimizing grace keep people from Jesus. It's not enough for us to offer grace or truth. We must offer both."

Far too many pulpits preach the love and grace of Christ at the expense of truth. Truth and grace are not in conflict with each other. They are interdependent on each other and both are necessary for Christians to lead others to eternity with Christ.

---

[42] John Calvin's Commentaries on St. Paul's Epistle to the Romans

[43] Alcorn, Randy, *The Grace and Truth Paradox*, Multnomah Publishers, Sisters Oregon, © 2003 by Eternal Perspective Ministries

Axis Powers

## **The Resistance (8.3)**

Jeremiah was a prophet who lived under five (5) different kings of Judah. One such king was Jehoiakim, a king who surrounded himself with "prophets" who would only tell him what he wanted to hear. Jeremiah spoke the truth and was the object ridicule and persecution by the false prophets who stood against him

**Jeremiah
1:16-17
18:18**

**Jeremiah
19:14-15
20:1-2**

**Jeremiah
23:16-30
26:11-15**

Jeremiah's message was painful to the people of Judah. It was a call to repentance and a call to judgement. It was also a message that the other "prophets" rejected.

Jeremiah was given a choice: Obey God and endure the persecution of the people; or disobey God and seek a peaceful coexistence with the other "prophets" of his day.

In Germany, the church had to make a choice – adoption of Nazi philosophy meant safety and security. Rejection of that philosophy meant persecution.

Aryan Paragraph (8)

## **Outcasts (8.4)**

For many years, American Christians have largely been insulated from the persecution that has existed around the world for centuries. In one sense, our freedom has generated a church that has greatly influenced the world for Christ.

In another sense, insulation from the war may have dulled our senses to a point of false security. We have become comfortable in our position in society. Comfort and security can lead to complacency while persecution will often breed urgency.

From the following passages what should we expect our position in society to be?

**Matthew 5:11-12** _____
**Matthew 24:5-14** _____
_____
_____

**2 Timothy 3:12-15** _____
_____
_____

America has devolved from a society with values derived from Christian ethics to a place where Christians are tolerated (seen but not heard). But even that "tolerance" is waning. At the present rate of moral degradation, it is only a matter of time – a very short time before Christians will face unmitigated persecution.

Will Christians adopt the Aryan paragraph in order to protect our security or will we stand with Christ?

## Axis Powers

# Special Orders (8.5)

Holland and Germany shared a common border. In an effort to protect her people Queen Wilhelmina of Holland sought to peacefully coexist with the Nazis. In her radio address in May, 1940, the Queen reassured her people that Hitler would not attack Holland. In less than 24 hours Germany began bombing her country. Her nation fell in five (5) days, and the Queen escaped to Britain where she worked with Allies to free her country from the Nazi oppression.

During the subsequent Nazi occupation, Casper ten Boom and his family began helping Jews who were under Nazi persecution. Casper ten Boom was a watch maker who, along with his daughters, Corrie and Betsie fashioned a "hiding place" to care for Jewish families who were in danger of persecution, imprisonment, and execution at the hands of an evil enemy.

During the Nazi occupation, the Nazis had ordered that all Jews be required to wear the Star of David, prominently displayed on their clothing, in order to make them more readily identifiable for persecution.

After the orders were given, Casper ten Boom, who was not Jewish himself, proudly wore the Star of David on his own clothing. When his daughters asked him why he took this action, he told them he preferred to be identified with God's chosen people:

> "I am too old for prison life, but if that were to happen, then **it would be, for me, an honor to give my life for God's ancient people, the Jews**" [44]

Neville Chamberlain sought peace through appeasement of the enemy. Queen Wilhelmina assured her people they would be insulated from the war and the enemy responded by swallowing up her country. Churchill responded by saying that appeasement was like feeding an alligator hoping it would eat you last.

---

[44] ten Boom, Corrie, *The Hiding Place*, Bantam Books, New York, 1971

## Aryan Paragraph (8)

A large group of churches in Germany embraced the Aryan Paragraph, choosing "peaceful coexistence" with the enemy over truth, in much the same manner as reflected when Christ addressed the church at Thyatira (Revelation 2):

> "But I have this against you,
> that you tolerate that woman Jezebel, who calls herself a prophetess and is teaching and seducing my servants"

Believers are not called to make peace with the world or its culture. When Jesus said "For God so loved the world", he was referring to the people in the world who are held captive by its culture and its leader (Satan). The world culture itself is our enemy. There is no room for compromise.

> Christ called us to stand firm
> against the enemy, not to find ways to
> peacefully coexist, compromise with its
> value system, or to develop a
> "balanced" world and life view.

In the adopting the Aryan paragraph, the church in Germany "balanced" their belief set to the point of evicting Christ himself from their churches.

### Practical Faith

Complicity with the "world" goes much deeper than taking a public stand on moral issues. Many of us find it easy to post messages on social media or to take a public stand in a political forum.

The immediate danger for us is the influence that the world has on each of us in our own personal daily walk. We can find ourselves embracing the world's values and pursuing its promises in our own private lives – in the home, in the workplace, and in our communities. We see the devolution of culture "out there" without recognizing the inward changes that are taking place in our own hearts and minds.

## Axis Powers

**Living in fear**

The German church was complicit with Hitler because their future existence was threatened. Persecuted Christians around the globe fear for their very lives. Many stand firm in their faith. Some do not.

In the western world, where Christianity is still openly tolerated (at least for now), our fears are largely based on our fear of being socially ostracized or belittled for our faith.

We fight legislation that limits our freedom. We are frequently labeled for our stance on public issues. But the "persecution" we face in our culture is minor in comparison with the persecution experienced by other Christians around the globe.

**Why do we cower in fear of the world and its culture?**

> "The Lord brings the counsel of the nations to nothing; he frustrates the plans of the peoples. The counsel of the Lord stands forever, the plans of his heart to all generations."
> **Psalm 33:10-11**

The world is held captive by the evil one – Satan himself. Yet we know that Satan himself was defeated at the Cross. Because Satan has been defeated – the culture under his dominion has also been defeated. We have no reason to fear.

> "Why do the nations rage and the peoples plot in vain?
> The kings of the earth set themselves and the rulers take counsel together against the Lord and against his Anointed, saying, 'Let us burst their bonds apart and cast way their cords from us' He who sits in the heavens laughs; the Lord holds hem in derision"
> **Psalm 2:2-4**

# Fifth Column (9)

**The Fifth Column**

Ernest Hemmingway wrote a play called the "Fifth Column" in 1937. The play was about a war correspondent (Phillip Rawlings) who served as a secret agent in the Spanish Civil War. In the play, he captures the leader of a "fifth column" of traitors hiding within Madrid and, in doing so, saves the city from falling into Nationalist hands.

It was Hemingway's play, performed in New York in 1940, that popularized the term **"fifth column"**. [45]

The origin of the term came from a radio broadcast during the Spanish Civil War by pro-Franco General Emilio Mola who predicted that a "fifth column" of Franco sympathizers inside the city of Madrid, would join his force of four military columns positioned just outside the City and secure the victory.

In general terms, "Fifth Columnists" were traitors who acted secretly and subversively out of sympathy for an enemy of their own country. Their actions may be carried out overtly or in secret. Their actions usually take the form of misinformation, espionage, sabotage or propaganda.

---

[45] Note: A military column is a formation of troops in which they all follow one behind the other. The term "Fifth Column" was first used in the Spanish Civil war by General Emilio Mola.

# Axis Powers

**Hitler's Fifth Column**

During World War II, Hitler was effective in using Nazi sympathizers as a fifth column to weaken his opponents from inside their own borders. He successfully used his "Fifth Column" in France, Austria, Czechoslovakia and Norway, among others.

**Marshal Philippe Pétain (Vichy France)**

22 June 1940 France was divided under the Franco-German Armistice. Germany had occupied a large part of France and the armistice allowed the other part (Vichy France) to remain independent. But their independence came with strings attached.

Marshal Petain & Pierre Laval (Vichy France)

Under the leadership of Pierre Laval and Marshal Pétain, the Vichy region of France existed only through cooperation and complicity with Adolf Hitler. Pétain, a celebrated French general in World War I collaborated with the Nazi regime and adopted repressive measures against Jews and served as the head of Vichy France from 1940 to 1944.

After the war, Petain was convicted of treason and sentenced to death, , but his former protégé Charles de Gaulle commuted this to life imprisonment. He died in prison in 1951 at the age of 95.

# Fifth Column (9)

## Lord "Haw-Haw" – Great Britain

William Joyce (nicknamed "Lord Haw-Haw") was an American-born fascist politician who broadcast Nazi propaganda to Britain during the World War II.

Born in Brooklyn, New York, Joyce moved to England with his father and mother in 1921 where he joined the Nazi movement in the mid-1930s.

Joyce was short tempered and gained a reputation as a street fighter. One of his altercations with a group of "Jewish Communists" resulted in a prominent scar that ran down the right side of his face from the lobe of his ear to the corner of his mouth. Every time he looked in the mirror he was reminded of his hatred of "the enemy".

Shortly before the war broke out in 1939, Joyce fled to Germany and became a broadcaster for the Nazi Propaganda Ministry. There, he regularly broadcast Nazi messages back to England from 1939 to 1945.

On the night of 30 April 30, a drunken Joyce made his last broadcast from Hamburg as Allied troops entered the city. Even in the face of certain defeat, Joyce remained committed to the Nazi cause. He rambled on through his farewell speech on the same night Hitler was saying good-bye to his entourage in anticipation of ending his life a few hours later.

On 3 January 1946, Joyce was convicted of treason by the British as a result of his wartime activities and went to the gallows unrepentant.

## Vidkun Quisling (Norway)

Quisling was Norwegian politician who seized power on 9 April 1940 in a Nazi-backed coup that led to the word "quisling" becoming synonymous with "traitor".

As one of World War II's most infamous traitors, He held the office of Minister President of Norway from 1 February 1942, to the end

# Axis Powers

of the war, while the elected leaders of Norway were exiled in London. Quisling was arrested on 9 May 1945, and was subsequently convicted of treason and executed by firing squad.

## Sudetenland

One of the provisions of the Treaty of Versailles at the end of World War I required Germany to give parcels of land on what was known as the Rhineland (bordering France) as well as land bordering Germany, Austria, and Czechoslovakia, known as the Sudetenland. This region was populated by Czechs, Slovaks, Poles, Hungarians, and Germans.

After taking back the Rhineland in 1936, Hitler set his sights on Austria and forced an election in March, 1938 that ended with their annexation into Germany. Hitler promised this would be the end of his expansion and, fearing war, other countries decided not to push back. Hitler lied.

Six months later, Hitler made his demand for the Sudetenland and, in September 1938, the allies (with Neville Chamberlain) signed the Munich agreement granting that region to Germany on the provision that Hitler would not invade Czechoslovakia. Hitler lied again.

Hitler went into the Sudetenland with help of anti-Semitic propaganda by Germans living in the region. The Great Depression had a significant impact on workers in Czechoslovakia and the Jews were a convenient scape-goat on which to place the blame for their problems. The Czech government made multiple attempts to appease Hitler including the suspension of Jewish teachers and dissolution of the Communist party.

On 15 March 1939, Hitler threatened a bombing raid against the Czech capital of Prague. The Czech president offered no resistance and by evening on the same day, Hitler made his triumphal entry into Prague.

# Fifth Column (9)

### Hitler's Fifth Column

"Fifth Column" tactics have been used in wars for centuries. Hitler was not the originator of the concept. However, he was certainly one of the most effective. He was particularly effective in countries with weaker leaders.

Pierre Laval and Marshal Pétain were in outright collusion with Hitler in his attempts to take control of France. The same was true of Norway and Vidkun Quisling.

Czechoslovakia, Austria, Norway, Denmark and the Netherlands put up very little resistance. Poland and France put up some resistance but both countries fell to Hitler quickly in the face of his show of military force. In almost every country conquered by Hitler, he had an organized group of sympathizers who were undermining the strength of their own country.

While Great Britain had its share of Nazi sympathizers and collaborators, Prime Minister Churchill and other leaders proved themselves to be the strong force in terms of will and determination. In the face of Nazi bombings of their country, they refused to capitulate even while Luftwaffe planes were bombing the city of London.

The fifth column tactic is less effective in places where there is a strong resolution to fight back.

| Axis Powers

## **The Enemy in the Mirror (9.1)**

"In man there are two conflicting principles, each of which strives for mastery. It is impossible for them to live together in peaceful coexistence. One principle is carnal; the other is spiritual...Our wills have the responsibility of choosing whether the carnal or the spiritual shall have ascendancy"
**J Oswald Sanders** [46]

**Romans 7:** Note what the Apostle calls a "war" (verse 23), that is taking him captive from within.

**Romans 7:1-6** _____
**Romans 7:17-19** _____
_____

**Romans 7:21-24** _____
**Romans 8:1-3** _____
_____

**Romans 8:7-8** _____
**Romans 8:11** _____
_____

Consider the warning of Charles Spurgeon:

> "Beware of no man more than yourself;
> we carry our worst enemies within us"

"But I say, walk by the Spirit, and you will not gratify the desires of the flesh. [17] For the desires of the flesh are against the Spirit, and the desires of the Spirit are against the flesh, for these are opposed to each other". **Galatians 5:16**

---

[46] Sanders, J. Oswald, *Enjoying Intimacy with God*, Moody Press, Chicago, IL 1980

Fifth Column (9)

## **Pride (9.2)**

"There is one vice of which no man in the world is free; which everyone in the world loathes when he sees it in someone else; and of which hardly any people, except Christians ever imagine that they are guilty themselves...The essential vice, the utmost evil, is Pride. Unchastely anger, greed, drunkenness, and all that, are mere fleabites in comparison: it was through Pride that the devil became the devil:

**"Pride leads to every other vice:
it is the complete anti-God state of mind**

"....As long as you are proud you cannot know God. A proud man is always looking down on things and people; and, of course, as long as you are looking down, you cannot see something that is above you"

**C. S. Lewis** [47]

As you reflect on C.S. Lewis' statement, is there anything in your own flesh that meets his definition of pride?

_____

_____

_____

*"Pride is like a degenerative eye disease
that gradually blinds you. But its progress is so slow
that you don't even realize you're losing your
spiritual vision – until it's too late"*
**Steve Farrar** [48]

---

[47] Lewis, C.S. *Mere Christianity,* Macmillan, 1952

[48] Farrar, Steve, *Finishing Strong*, Multnomah Publishers, Sisters Oregon 1995)

| Axis Powers

## I did it my way (9.3)

In Daniel 4, King Nebuchadnezzar proclaimed the praises of God:

> "It has seemed good to me to show the signs and wonders that the most high God has done for me. How great are his signs, how mighty his wonders! His kingdom is an everlasting and his dominion endures from generation to generation"
>
> **Daniel 4:2-3**

Read **Daniel 4:29-33**: Contrast Nebuchadnezzar's attitude with his statement in Daniel 4:2-3. **What changed?**

_____
_____
_____


Note the struggle of Uzziah (King of Judah) in **2 Chronicles 26**:

_____
_____

From verses 16-23 what can we conclude about Uzziah?

_____
_____
_____

Prosperity can turn a heart from humble gratitude to sinful pride when the focus turns from God to ourselves.

Fifth Column (9)

## Self Sufficiency (9.4)

"The itch of self-regard craves the scratch of self-approval. That is, if we are getting our pleasure from feeling self-sufficient, we will not be satisfied without others' seeing and applauding our self-sufficiency"

**John Piper** [49]

We live in a world where the Bible is often treated as a collection of "one-liners" to be used in certain situations (sometimes appropriately, but often out of context). Two passages from 1 Peter regularly fit this characterization:

1 Peter 5:6-7 and 1 Peter 5:8-9 are often quoted separately and out of context. These passages are a part of the same paragraph (that also includes verse 10) in Peter's letter.

Read these passages in full context and see if the focal point changes

**1 Peter 1:1** _____

**1 Peter 1:13-14** _____

**1 Peter 2:11-12** _____

**1 Peter 4:1-3** _____

_____

**1 Peter 5:1-11** _____

---

[49] Piper, John, *Battling Unbelief*, 2007, Desiring God Foundation, Multnomah Books, Colorado Springs, Co

# Axis Powers

The Book of 1 Peter was Peter's letter to Christians who were under persecution. In Chapter 1 he reminds us of the blessings of being one of Christ's elect and calls us to focus our attention there instead of looking at our trials.

In Chapters 2 and 3, Peter calls us to forsake the flesh and to respond to a more righteous calling. In 1 Peter 2:5, he reminds us that we are living stones that are part of a spiritual house, and he leads us to verse 11 where he describes us as "sojourners and exiles" (*NASB* uses the terms "aliens and strangers"), calling us to abstain from the lusts of the flesh.

As we move into Chapter 5, Peter calls us to a lifestyle marked by humility. Humility is vital to our relationship with God. It is the lynchpin of a dependent lifestyle. In verse 5 he tells us that "God opposes the proud but gives grace to the humble". The message here is that humility and dependence are critical if we want His power to work in and through us.

The battle with the flesh begins and ends with dependence on Christ, His grace, and His Word. The phrase "He will exalt you/lift you up, in due time", is not about our own personal exaltation or victory. It is his reminder that our well-being is in his hands.

That phrase is part of a letter that is written so that, when the battle heats up, we will be encouraged to turn our hearts and minds to Christ for perseverance. Satan is on the prowl. We are under attack. But take heart, as we humble ourselves under God's mighty hand, he will engage the battle and lift us up in due time.

**As with Nebuchadnezzar in the previous section, when the focus turns to ourselves, we become easy prey for a hungry lion.**

Fifth Column (9)

# **The Resolution (9.5)**

Chick-fil-a has a well-known reputation for being closed on Sundays. If you read his biography, you will discover that Chick-fil-a founder, Truett Cathey, made a number of commitments to biblical precepts long before he made his first chicken sandwich.

Daniel, Hannaniah, Mishael and Azeriah had difficult choices to make under Nebuchadnezzar and other Babylonian kings.

**Daniel 1:8-14** _____

**Daniel 3:16-18** _____

How should a Believer respond to the Flesh?

**Colossians 3:1-8** _____

The voice of the flesh can be powerful and convincing. We can be sure that Mr. Cathey was not totally immune to temptation when others encouraged him to abandon his own beliefs. But Mr. Cathey made a resolution early in his life that served him well when he faced the temptation.

Scripture tells us that Shadrach, Meshach and Abednego did not hesitate when confronted by Nebuchadnezzar. They had settled that matter long before this confrontation. It was a line that they would not think of crossing.

Decisions made in the heat of the battle are often poor decisions. This is especially true with spiritual warfare. Daniel and his three friends had already settled their decision long before they were confronted by Nebuchadnezzar.

Axis Powers

## **Special Orders (9.6)**

"Hitler's "fifth column" so penetrated many governments of Europe that they collapsed at the first touch of war. Broadly speaking, this fifth column included men like Prime Minister Chamberlain and Premier Daladier, who weakened the defenses of their nations by destroying democracy in Spain and, later, by giving the Czech fortifications to Hitler, in order to tempt his armies eastward. It included American industrialists who sold scrap iron to Japan, and strengthened her against the USA. None of these people considered themselves traitors. Nor, probably, did Quisling and Laval and others who, with various excuses, took part in puppet governments serving the invader." [50]

Most of us will acknowledge Satan as our spiritual enemy. A smaller number will recognize the world as our enemy. However, as Christians we play host to an insidious enemy who is often effective in quenching the voice of the Holy Spirit and in turning our hearts and minds away from Christ himself.

**Satan's "Fifth Column" is our own flesh**, that part of the old self that continues to demand its own way, believe its own lies, to satisfy its own passions, and to worship its own idols.

"The world is no friend to grace; our own flesh strives against the spirit; but ultimately, there is no man-hating enemy of the soul like Satan. Although he has no immediate power over the mind and soul of the believer, **the devil knows how to use the world and how to play upon our fleshly propensities.** He is the exquisite tempter; he knows how to snare souls and cause Christians to doubt the mercy of God."

**Thomas Brooks**

---

[50] Strong, Anna Louise. *The Stalin Era.* New York: Mainstream, 1956

## Fifth Column (9)

In spiritual warfare, Satan's most effective accomplice is the flesh, his "Fifth Column".

As humans, it is very "normal" to trust our own flesh, our own mental capacity and reasoning skills and intuitions – even our own feelings and desires. But the flesh is not trustworthy. When confronted, the flesh is ready to fight. The flesh always wants to be in control and the old man in us has an insatiable appetite for idols, material possessions and self-exaltation. We need recognize the flesh as our enemy and prepare for its assault.

> "If I profess with the loudest voice
> and clearest exposition
> every portion of the truth of God
> except precisely that little point which the world and the
> devil at that moment are attacking, I am not confessing
> Christ, however boldly I may be professing Christ
>
> "Where the battle rages,
> there the loyalty of the soldier is proved,
> and to be steady on all the battlefield besides
> is mere flight and disgrace
> if he flinches at that point" [51]

Our culture is glutted with books and philosophies built around making excuses for sinful behavior. We blame our poor choices on so-called "natural instincts". We blame them on our circumstances or the acts of others. We justify, minimize or rationalize. In recent years there has been a heavy emphasis on improving "self-esteem". No matter how well intended, when we embrace "self-esteem", we are teaching ourselves self-worship.

---

[51] This quote is widely attributed to Martin Luther, but it is more likely from Elizabeth Rundle Charles, in a book called *The Chronicles of the Schoenberg-Cotta Family*, published in 1865.

## Axis Powers

For reasons we cannot fully understand, it seems that, when we first become a Christian, God addresses some parts of our sinful nature and deals with them decisively. But he allows other parts of our sin nature to persist for a time, allowing us to grow through the process of wresting with the remnants of our old nature. What part of the "old nature" continually seeks to draw you away from Christ?

- o Pride
- o Self-sufficiency
- o Fears (real or imagined)
- o Desire for the praise of others
- o Bitterness
- o Greed
- o Gossip
- o Sexual desires
- o Covetousness
- o Anger / Resentment
- o Other?

Secular therapies offer "self-help" solutions to help us deal with our "inappropriate" decisions and actions. Most are directed at making you feel better about yourself. The only effective cure for the flesh is a heart transplant. We are called to "crucify the flesh" and replace with the Holy Spirit:

> "... walk by the Spirit, and you will not gratify the desires of the flesh. For the **desires of the flesh are against the Spirit**, and the desires of the Spirit are against the flesh ...[19] Now the works of the flesh are evident: sexual immorality, impurity, sensuality, idolatry, sorcery, enmity, strife, jealousy, fits of anger, rivalries, dissensions, divisions, envy drunkenness, orgies, and things like these. ... [22] But the fruit of the Spirit is love, joy, peace, patience, kindness, goodness, faithfulness, gentleness, self-control; against such things there is no law. And those who belong to Christ Jesus have crucified the flesh with its passions and desires"
> **Galatians 5:16-24**

# Fifth Column (9)

> "If God puts something in my hand without first doing something to my heart, my character will lag behind my achievements, and that is the way to ruin"
> **Warren Wiersbe** [52]

The flesh is Satan's "Fifth Column". The old man in the mirror is not our friend. He seeks to medicate his own ego and gratify his own desires. He wants to be in control and his needs always come first. Even in his "good deeds", there is usually a desire for reward or recognition.

Perhaps you are reading this paragraph and asking "Are we really that bad?" The answer to that question is "yes" – apart from the inward work of the Holy Spirit, our flesh is totally depraved. Even the Apostle Paul recognized this fact when he, in Romans 7 referred to himself as a "wretched man" in need of a rescue from "this body of death".

When we hear that inner voice calling us to action we need to know the source. Our consciences can be seared and our emotions can take control. When the voice inside of us speaks to us, we should ask for identification. When the Holy Spirit speaks, He never contradicts the Scripture that He wrote.

Scripture calls us to **CRUCIFY** the flesh. It says nothing about minor adjustments or modifications. The flesh is just as much a spiritual enemy as Satan himself. He cannot be trusted. The battle with the flesh is a battle for the heart. Either we desire to serve God or we serve the enemy.

---

[52] from *Finishing Strong*, by Steve Farrar – Multinomah Publishers, Sisters, Oregon 1995

| Axis Powers

# Operation Himmler (10)

## 1 September 1939 – 4:45 AM

Excerpts from History.com [53]
"1.5 million German troops invade Poland all along its 1,750-mile border with German-controlled territory. Simultaneously, the German Luftwaffe bombed Polish airfields, and German warships and U-boats attacked Polish naval forces in the Baltic Sea. Nazi leader Adolf Hitler claimed the massive invasion was a defensive action, but Britain and France were not convinced. On September 3, they declared war on Germany, initiating World War II."

Alfred Naujocks

Germany annexed Austria on 12 March 1938 and Czechoslovakia a year later on 15 March 1939. Both were accomplished without igniting hostilities with the major powers, and Hitler hoped that his invasion of Poland would likewise be tolerated.

On 23 August, 1939, Germany signed a non-aggression pact with the Soviet Union in order to keep them from coming to Poland's aid, but Britain had already promised to support Poland in the event of an attack.

---

[53] History.com – "Germans Invade Poland", 4 March 2010, A&E Television Networks.

## Operation Himmler (10)

Hitler wanted Poland. To that end, he fully expected appeasement from France and Britain in much the same way they had in Czechoslovakia and Austria. Instead, both countries responded by declaring war on Germany, thus setting the stage for the official start of World War II.

Hitler began a propaganda and misinformation campaign against Poland in order to justify his planned actions and in order to rally support among the German people. His plan was code-named "Operation Himmler":

> "At 8 p.m. on August 31, Nazi S.S. troops wearing Polish uniforms staged a phony invasion of Germany, damaging several minor installations on the German side of the border. They also left behind a handful of dead concentration camp prisoners in Polish uniforms to serve as further evidence of the supposed Polish invasion, which Nazi propagandists publicized as an unforgivable act of aggression." [54]

**Operation Himmler:**

Heinrich Himmler headed up Hitler's Schutzstaffel (S.S.) and Reinhard Heydrich was head of the Nazi Party Intelligence (Sicherheitsdienst / S.D.). Both men were among Hitler's most trusted and were effective in carrying out even the most heinous and complex orders from Hitler.

Heydrich had devised a scheme to give Hitler his justification for an attack on Poland. Several border incidents would be created, under what was called "Operation Himmler". An elite unit under the leadership of Alfred Naujocks would capture the radio tower at Gleiwitz, Poland along the border then broadcast anti-Nazi Polish propaganda into the Reich.

Naujocks and his team traveled to the town and checked into a hotel, claiming to be engineers looking for suitable materials to mine in the area. Hitler postponed the invasion until 1 September

---

[54] Ibid

# Axis Powers

1939. Naujocks and his men waited at Gleiwitz for the order to proceed.

In order to bolster the impact of the propaganda, "Operation Canned Goods" was hatched wherein a small skirmish was staged near the radio tower. Heinrich Muller, the head of the Gestapo, had several concentration-camp inmates shot or drugged and their bodies transported to the area. With Polish army uniforms and pay books, the former camp prisoners now appeared to be Polish casualties of the battle.

On 31 August 1939, Naujocks took his squad into the radio station. There, he found the two men on duty ready and compliant. The Polish speaker then yelled a short tirade into the microphone calling for war to begin between Poland and Germany. The squad then ran outside, firing off their pistols as they went.

### Hitler's Speech to the Reichstag [55]

"As always, I attempted to bring about, by the peaceful method of making proposals for revision, an alteration of this intolerable position. It is a lie when the outside world says that we only tried to carry through our revisions by pressure... You know the endless attempts I made for a peaceful clarification and understanding of the problem of Austria, and later of the problem of the Sudetenland, Bohemia, and Moravia. It was all in vain...

"This night for the first time Polish regular soldiers fired on our territory. Since 5.45 A.M. we have been returning the fire, and from now on bombs will be met by bombs. Whoever fight with poison gas will be fought with poison gas. Whoever departs from the rules of humane warfare can only expect that we shall do the same. I will continue this struggle, no matter against whom, until the safety of the Reich and its rights are secured."

---

[55] Address by Adolf Hitler, Chancellor of the Reich, before the Reichstag, September 1, 1939

Operation Himmler (10)

In his speech to the Reichstag, Hitler formally declared war on Poland, citing the various border incidents and Gleiwitz in particular as "frontier violations of a nature no longer tolerable for a great power."

The same speech made references to his quest for peaceful resolutions, a commitment not to harm women and children and a call for Germans to stand with him in his noble fight.

The attack on Gleiwitz and subsequent speech just another criminal act and deception in a long line of lies perpetrated by Hitler and his regime.

### Blitzkrieg

Germany used its "blitzkrieg" (lightning war) and the air support of the Luftwaffe to overwhelm the Polish army – reaching Warsaw in just 8 days.

On 17 September 1939, the Soviet Union invaded Poland to secure its territory. The next day Poland's government and military leaders fled the country. Poland surrendered on 28 September 1939.

### Enemy's Masquerade

Germany's 18-day war against Poland began with a ruse wherein Germans staged a Polish attack against German citizens along the border – and published that attack in newsreels to the German people. The result was a common hatred and support of Hitler's brutality against Polish citizens. **Through his elaborate masquerade, Hitler was effective in persuading the German people to defend themselves against an enemy that did not exist.**

| Axis Powers

## **Satan's Fodder (10.1)**

There are many in the visible Church who have never truly placed their faith and trust in Jesus Christ as Lord and Savior. Indeed, there are many who demonstrate knowledge of Christian teachings without having come to a personal relationship with Christ.

There are also true Believers in the Church who walk by the flesh more often than by the Spirit. Satan is skilled in using both to his advantage in order to turn others away from Christ.

Besides true Christians, what other types of people do we see in the Church and how are we called to respond?

**Matthew 13:24-30**

**Matthew 13:36-43**

**Matthew 13:47-50**

The parable of the weeds (above) shows us that God has chosen to allow non-believers to exist within the community of professing Christians – to be sorted out and dealt with in His own time.

The visible Church includes many who have not made a true profession of faith. Some join the church for social or political reasons. Others may be sincere in their search for life's answers and have joined the church without truly turning their lives over to Christ in repentance and faith. For some, Christianity is a type of "therapy" to help cope with life's challenges.

Still others have joined the Church for the purposes of disrupting or altering its message.

## Operation Himmler (10)

In the book of Acts, we see members of the visible church active in ministry. Some are sincerely seeking to engage and others have less noble motivations.

**Acts 19:11-19**
**Acts 20:29-30**

From Satan's perspective, the mixed message of the visible Church is a weakness to be exploited. The world and Satan will often point to divisions and inconsistencies within the visible Church as "evidence" through which they can attack the Church and its message.

Our call is to be the salt and light to the world and still manage the weeds among us. It is a challenge that can, if we take advantage, strengthen us in our faith. From a purely evangelistic perspective, the "weeds" among us represent opportunities to win them over to Christ.

Winning this battle will require knowledge of and unwavering devotion to the truth as revealed in Scripture.

## A battle indeed.

## Axis Powers

# Hypocrisy (10.2)

"Of all the things in the world that stink in the nostrils of an honest man, hypocrisy is the worst. If you are worldling, be a worldling. If you serve Satan, serve him. If Baal is god, serve him, but do not mask your service of self and sin by a pretended service to God. Appear to be what you are, tear off the masks. The church was never meant to be a masquerade...when a man has a divided heart, to serve God and to serve Satan at the same time; I say his disease is of such a loathsome and degraded character that the very worldling whose leprosy is on his brow, despises, hates and avoids him"

**Charles Spurgeon** [56]

**Mark 7:5-8** – What was Jesus saying about the issue of hypocrisy?

**Matthew 23** – What was Jesus' message to the Pharisees?

True followers of Christ will often stumble. The world and Satan are quick to seize on the opportunity to brand us as hypocrites when our walk is antithetical to our message as image bearers of Christ. But hypocrisy is just one of the many sins that we are called to repent from and deal with. We can deny it, excuse, defend it, minimize it – or we can confess it and deal ruthlessly with it.

As Spurgeon said: **Hypocrisy stinks!**

---

[56] Pierce, Larry & Marion, *The Spurgeon Series 1859 & 1860*, Attic Books, Green Forest, Arkansas 2012

Operation Himmler (10)

## **The Believer's Response (10.3)**

"Christ also suffered for you, leaving you an example, so that you might follow in his steps… 23 When he was reviled, he did not revile in return; when he suffered, he did not threaten, but continued entrusting himself to him who judges justly."

**1 Peter 2: 21-23**

In Romans 12:3, Paul reminds us that, because of grace we should not think more highly of ourselves.

**Romans 12:9-21**: Study this passage and note the character traits that should define us as image bearers of Christ.

When Christians excuse bad behavior by pointing to the fact that "we are sinners saved by grace", what the world often sees is a group of people who issue a haughty condemnation of their behavior while excusing their own. While it is theologically accurate that saving grace only applies to followers of Christ, the optics of dismissing our own sin while condemning theirs leaves us open to the label of hypocrite.

The answer to accusations of hypocrisy lies not in the demonstration of our perfection but in **demonstration** of the grace that we verbally proclaim.

Axis Powers

## A Religion of Hate (10.4)

"It is easier to hide behind philosophical arguments, heavily footnoted for effect, than it is to admit our hurts, our confusions, our loves, and our passions in the marketplace of life's heartfelt transactions."

**Ravi Zacharias**

**Mark 2:14-17** – While Pharisees are busy distancing themselves from sinners, what was Jesus doing?

**Luke 19:1-10**

Comment on Jesus' purpose and motive in these encounters.

Professing Christians (true Believers and imposters) are often branded for actions taken in public forums. While many of those fights are rooted in righteous indignation, our tactics, methods, and words are often seen (sometimes justifiably so) as hateful and vitriolic.

We often walk a fine line in standing firm for the truth while proclaiming a Gospel rooted in the love and grace of Christ.

We are called to demonstrate the love of Christ to people who need him without compromising the truth that promises to set them free. The battle requires engagement, compassion, empathy, love, and a desire to serve people who don't know Christ, all without compromising the truth of sin, judgement, hell, the necessity of repentance and the exclusivity of the Gospel message

Operation Himmler (10)

## Special Orders (10.5)

We live in a world where Christians are branded as hate-filled hypocrites standing in harsh judgment of others with our message of exclusivity and what they brand as bigotry. They contend that our Bible is filled with lies and contradictions and our Savior was just a good man or prophet like Buddha, Mohammed, or one of many other teachers.

Satan masquerades as an "Angel of Light" – convincing the world and the flesh that the messages of Scripture, the message and actions of the Church, and most professing Christians themselves are, in fact, the enemies. He offers a counterfeit religion where there is universal acceptance and where all forms of behavior (except Christianity) are celebrated.

Satan's attacks are to be expected. Believers have the capacity to reinforce Satan's deception or counter his message with the truth of the gospel – not only in our words, but also in our actions.

This battle will not be won in the political arena, in our schools, in the courthouse or in business or social circles, although our influences on those battlegrounds are important. The battle is entirely spiritual and can only be won if hearts are radically changed.

Satan's deceptions have persuaded many to trust him while creating the illusion that Christians are the enemy. He has effectively used the world and its culture to join him in his attacks. We will win this battle only by winning the hearts of those held captive by Satan's deception.

Satan is skilled in his deception. The world is complicit because they believe in his message. Our own flesh is continually at work turning our actions and words to benefit the enemy.

Satan has declared war on Christ and his followers. Christ has promised victory. He has promised that the "gates of hell" will not prevail against his Church. But we should not be surprised at the trials, opposition, and persecution that have come our way and that will continue to come.

# Axis Powers

In **John 15:18-19**, Jesus warns us:

> "If the world hates you, know that it has hated me before it hated you. If you were of the world, the world would love you as its own; but because you are not of the world, but I chose you out of the world, therefore the world hates you"

While we should expect the world to hate us, Jesus has called us to respond in a way that exhibits grace and truth. We will never stop the world from hating the Church – but our winsome presentation of the Gospel will lead many of them to turn to Christ.

## The Pharisee

In Matthew 23, Jesus made it very clear that the Pharisees' attitudes toward others was the very antithesis of grace and the polar opposite of what Jesus, himself demonstrated.

The hypocritical Pharisees would never consider being seen with the tax collectors and sinners of their day. They saw the "sinner" as someone unworthy to be seen with, let alone to dine with or to care for. Their attitude was one of arrogant condemnation, exalting themselves as righteous while holding others to the smallest detail of the law.

## Scandalous Grace

In Mark 2, we read about Jesus' encounter with a tax collector named Levi (Matthew). Luke 19 reveals another meeting between Jesus and a tax collector (Zacchaeus). Jesus met with them, ate with them, and engaged them at a personal level. Matthew was called as a disciple. Zacchaeus repented and his life was changed.

In John 4, Jesus met a Samaritan woman who was entangled in an immoral lifestyle. Jesus' very conversation with her was "scandalous" for that day. A Jewish man speaking to a Samaritan woman! But the conversation went deeply into her personal life in a way that graciously and lovingly addressed her sin and brought her to repentance.

Jesus actively involved himself in the lives of non-believers. Through grace and compassion, He changed their lives in the process. He preached and demonstrated grace without compromising truth.

**Scalia and Ginsberg**

Justices Ruth Bader Ginsberg (a Jewish liberal) and Antonin Scalia (A conservative Roman Catholic) were polar opposites in their interpretation of the United States Constitution. These are her words following Justice Scalia's death in 2016:

> "We are different, we are one, different in our interpretation of written texts, one in our reverence for the Constitution and the institution we serve. From our years together at the D.C. Circuit, we were best buddies. We disagreed now and then, but when I wrote for the Court and received a Scalia dissent, the opinion ultimately released was notably better than my initial circulation.
>
> "Justice Scalia nailed all the weak spots — the 'apple-sauce' and 'argle bargle'—and gave me just what I needed to strengthen the majority opinion. He was a jurist of captivating brilliance and wit, with a rare talent to make even the most sober judge laugh"

Although Justice Scalia rarely won Justice Ginsberg over politically, his conduct in their relationship often influenced her thought process. We can learn from their example. Although they were fierce competitors on the Bench, the respect they showed for each other demonstrated a common grace that kept barriers from forming.

**The Challenge**

> "When they had set a day for Paul, they came to him at his lodging in large numbers; and he was explaining to them by solemnly testifying about the kingdom of God and trying to persuade them concerning Jesus, from both the Law of Moses and from the Prophets, from morning until evening. **Some were being persuaded by the things spoken, but others would not believe**"
>
> **Acts 28:23-24**

## Axis Powers

When we enter the debate over ideology, we should examine our own hearts and settle the important question of motivation:

> "Are we more interested in winning a debate with an ideological enemy, or are we truly interested in winning them over to Christ?"

Satan works diligently to misrepresent Christ and his followers. Christians are called to be image bearers of Christ. Love and grace are not antithetical to truth. We can easily err in either direction: abandon truth in the name of grace; or use the truth like a club in a misguided attempt to beat them into submission.

We are on a rescue mission. Our challenge is to speak the truth and still demonstrate the grace and love that defines us as followers of Christ.

> "Your life
> as a Christian should make
> non-believers question their
> disbelief in God"
> **Dietrich Bonhoeffer**

Operation Himmler (10)

# Allied Powers

Every Christian is called to
"fight the good fight of faith"
and to persevere in spiritual battle.
But none of us are called to stand alone.

The United States, Britain, Canada, Australia, the
Soviet Union, France and others
came together as Allied Powers in
World War II to defeat an evil
and powerful enemy.

For Christians, victory has already
been secured through Christ's
finished work on the Cross. Our daily spiritual
battles are fought through
the equipping power of the Holy Spirit and
armed by his amazing Grace.

| Allied Powers

# Persecution (11)

"Our epoch will certainly see the end of the disease of Christianity. It will last another hundred years, two hundred perhaps. My regret will have been that I couldn't, like whoever the prophet as, behold the promised land from afar. We are entering into a conception of the world that will be a sunny era, an **era of tolerance**." [57]

**Adolf Hitler**

Enemies of Christianity have aggressively attempted to link Christianity with Hitler, asserting that he and other Nazis were either Christians or influenced by Christianity. Nothing could be further from the truth. Nazi attitude toward Christianity was unambiguously hostile.

"What is this God who takes pleasure only in seeing men grovel before Him? Try to picture to yourselves the meaning of the following, quite simple story. God creates the conditions for sin. Later on He succeeds, with the help of the Devil, in causing man to sin. Then He employs a virgin to bring into the world a son who, by His death, will redeem humanity!"[58]

**Adolf Hitler**

The Nazi level of tolerance for the Church was only a question of political strategy, not rooted in belief or ideology. Germany was a nation of "cultural Christians", both Protestant and Roman

---

[57] Trevor-Roper, Hugh, ed (2000). Hitler's Table Talk 1941-1944. Trans. N. Cameron and R.H. Stevens New York: Enigma Books

[58] Ibid: 13 December 1941

## Persecution (11)

Catholic. Any sudden and overt attack on the church would not be well received by the German people. The Nazi strategy with respect to the church was designed to minimize their interference with the Nazi cause.

> "The religion fabricated by Paul of Tarsus, which was later called Christianity, is nothing but the Communism of today."[59]
>
> **Adolf Hitler**

There were many members of the Nazi hierarchy who were overtly hostile to Christianity and felt that outright persecution was the best way to deal with those who refused to accept the "new order." Others wanted to avoid stirring up unnecessary hostility that might weaken popular support for the government.

They felt that Christianity was doomed to die out on its own and the wisest policy was to strictly control the church, forbid dissention, and concentrate on winning the youth.

### Holocaust

As a whole, Christians were not subjected to the level of persecution that Hitler inflicted on the Jewish people. The visible church in Germany operated under the authority of the German government and had the choice of compliance or persecution and extinction at the hands of Adolf Hitler.

There is no question that many churches in Nazi Germany stood silent during the Holocaust. Many joined in Jewish persecution through acceptance of the "Aryan Paragraph". Some even replaced the Bible with Mien Kampf in their pulpits and disavowed the Old Testament, altogether. Their actions will stand as a blight on the record of the organized church in Germany.

But many Christians (Bother Protestant and Roman Catholic), who publicly opposed the Nazi ideology. Much has been written of the works of Dietrich Bonhoeffer, Karl Barth, Bishop Martin Niemoller and others who stood in opposition to Hitler. Niemoller

---

[59] Trevor-Roper Night of 29 November 1944

# Allied Powers

spent seven (7) years in solitary confinement in a Nazi concentration camp, and Bonhoeffer was arrested and executed shortly before the end of the war.

> "When blood, race, nationality and honor are regarded as eternal values, then the first commandment obliges the Christian to refuse this valuation. When the Aryan is glorified, the Word of God teaches that all men are sinful. If the Christian is forced by the Anti-Semitism of the Nazi Weltanschauung to hate the Jew, he is, on the contrary, bidden by the Christian commandment to love his neighbor."
>
> *1936 Statement from the Confessing Church, Whitsie, Germany*

## Persecution of the Church

The Nazi strategy of persecution included the systematic campaign for the suppression of denominational and youth organizations, a campaign against denominational schools, and a defamation campaign against the clergy, all starting on the same day in the whole area of the Reich. These campaigns were supported by the entire regimented press, by Nazi Party meetings, by traveling party speakers.

> "The megalomaniac required absolute loyalty to himself. He would share no room in the souls of men with God. Hitler's plan was the establishment of the First Church of National Socialism, and since true Christianity would stand in the way, Hitler declared war on the church as well as the world."
>
> **Joel Miller** [60]

In April, 1933, Jehovah's Witnesses were banned as an organization because of their beliefs. Their literature was confiscated, and they lost their jobs, unemployment benefits, pensions, and all social welfare benefits. Many were sent to prisons and concentration camps in Nazi Germany, and their children were sent to juvenile detention homes and orphanages.

---

[60] Miller, Joel, Hitler's War on Christ, www.worldnetdaily.com, January 12, 2002

## Persecution (11)

> This ban sent a clear message to all
> religious groups in Germany
> **"consent or face consequences"**.

Some of the measures taken by the Nazi government to limit the activities of the churches (and hasten their demise) included:
- Arrest and incarceration (in concentration camps) of non-compliant clergy;
- Physical assaults on clergy were ignored by police;
- Faith based academic, social, athletic, professional and youth organizations were banned;
- Church literature was censored;
- Church property (including orphanages, schools, hospitals, etc.) was seized; religious insignias were removed, and teachers fired;
- Public meetings were forbidden unless approved by the government;
- Attacks on Christianity in the press;
- Religious activities were restricted to church buildings only;
- Surveillance of worship services and church leaders;
- Civil servants were required to withdraw their children from religious youth organizations;
- Church criticism of the government was forbidden;
- Prayers were forbidden at school assemblies;
- Crucifixes and religious paintings were removed from schools;
- Many independent religious groups were banned completely and organization of new groups was prohibited;
- Churches were not allowed to have a voice in political matters – under the definition of "separation of church and state";
- High school teachers were forbidden to be active in religious youth groups;

Allied Powers

"A lot of people will say, 'I didn't realize that they were trying to convert Christians to a Nazi philosophy,'. They wanted to eliminate the Jews altogether, but they were also looking to eliminate Christianity."

**Julie Seltzer Mandel** [61]

"Our epoch will certainly see the end of the disease of Christianity"
## Adolf Hitler

Christians did not endure the persecution of the Holocaust in any way comparable to Jews. Hitler sought the extinction of Jews as an "undesirable race". For strategic reasons his attacks on Christianity took a subtler and longer term plan. He recognized the fact that Christianity was a threat to his power base, but he feared losing the support of the German people. His attacks on the Church were deliberate and methodical, with the ultimate goal being the extinction of Christianity altogether.

"There are times when we not only may but must disobey earthly authorities. Whenever the earthly authority commands us to do something God forbids, or forbids us from doing something God commands, it is our duty to disobey the earthly authorities."

**R. C. Sproul**

**Religion of Hitler?**
Critics of Christianity regularly a persistently identify Hitler as a "Christian" by pointing to his public claims of his providential and "God-ordained" mission. However, standing in front of a crowd and shouting "Vrooom!" will not make you a car.

---

[61] Nuremberg Project for the Rutgers Journal of Law and Religion

## Persecution (11)

In the myriad of public speeches where Hitler claims his destiny, he regularly invoked the name of God and Jesus while drawing attention to his own mission of persecution. He quoted the words of Jesus – **but only when Jesus was dealing with the Pharisees**. Those words were used to justify his antisemitism and his claim that Jesus was not Jewish.

> "My feeling as a Christian points me to my Lord and Savior as a fighter.... In boundless love as a Christian and as a man I read through the passage which tells us how the Lord at last rose in His might and seized the scourge to drive out of the Temple the brood of vipers and adders. How terrific was his fight against the Jewish poison." [62]
>
> **Adolf Hitler**

In his Papal Encyclical, "*With Burning Concern*", Pope Pius XI confronted Hitler for his elevation of himself and the Aryan race above God.

With all of his public speeches invoking the name of God, the Nazi ideal attempted to take over the church, categorically denied the entire Old Testament and Hitler regularly denied the Apostolic authority of Paul. Take inventory of that statement. Of 66 books in the Bible, Hitler denied 39 (Old Testament). 13 New Testament epistles were written by Paul and the book of Acts is largely devoted to Paul's missionary journeys. That leaves 14 out 66 that he might agree with – until you erase all of Jesus' references to the Old Testament....

**NO. Adolf Hitler was not a Christian
nor even a distant cousin of Christianity.**

---

[62] Baynes, Norman H. (1942). The Speeches of Adolf Hitler: April 1922-August 1939. 1. New York: Oxford University Press

Allied Powers

## **Survivors**

Christians who fought alongside their Jewish brothers found themselves in the middle of intense persecution, torture, imprisonment, and death at the hands of Hitler's followers. Many Christians and Jews died waiting on the defeat of Nazi Germany.

America's involvement in World War II lasted less than 4 years. For survivors of Nazi persecution, it lasted much longer, beginning with the 30 January 1933 appointment of Adolf Hitler as Chancellor of Germany. Yet, even with the death of Hitler and the surrender of Germany in 1945, their time of endurance was not yet over:

> "For (Jewish) survivors, returning to life as it had been before the Holocaust was impossible. Jewish communities no longer existed in much of Europe. When people tried to return to their homes from camps or hiding places, they found that, in many cases, their homes had been looted or taken over by others....

> "Many survivors ended up in displaced persons' (DP) camps set up in western Europe under Allied military occupation at the sites of former concentration camps. There they waited to be admitted to places like the United States, South Africa, or Palestine. At first, many countries continued their old immigration policies, which greatly limited the number of refugees they would accept. The British government, which controlled Palestine, refused to let large numbers of Jews in. Many Jews tried to enter Palestine without legal papers, and when caught some were held in camps on the island of Cyprus, while others were deported back to Germany. ..."[63]

---

[63] United States Holocaust Memorial Museum, ushmm.org , "The Survivors"

Persecution (11)

## The Long Wait Was Over

"...Finally, the United Nations voted to divide Palestine into a Jewish and Arab state. Early in 1948, the British began withdrawing from Palestine. On 14 May 1948, one of the leading voices for a Jewish homeland, David Ben-Gurion, announced the formation of the State of Israel. After this, Jewish refugee ships freely landed in the seaports of the new nation. he United States also changed its immigration policy to allow more Jewish refugees to enter.

"Although many Jewish survivors were able to build new lives in their adopted countries, many non-Jewish victims of Nazi policies continued to be persecuted in Germany. Laws which discriminated against Roma (Gypsies) continued to be in effect until 1970 in some parts of the country. The law used in Nazi Germany to imprison homosexuals remained in effect until 1969." [64]

## The Spiritual War

In Genesis 3:15, God spoke to Satan and said: "I will put enmity between you and the woman and between your offspring and her offspring, and he shall bruise your head and you shall bruise his heel.

Spiritual warfare began in the garden and God's people began their wait for the woman's offspring to make His entry into the world.

Centuries later, the wait was over.
God fulfilled his promise in a humble stable in Bethlehem.

---

[64] Ibid

# Prophecy (11.1)

A portion of the Old Testament was written in Aramaic, while the primary language was Hebrew. In the second and third centuries B.C., the Old Testament was translated into Greek, the common language of the day, into what is called the "Septuagint".

Understanding the various paths that the original languages took from Hebrew and Aramaic to Greek, Latin, and our modern English translations is a study in and of itself.

The important point to understand here is that Old Testament prophecies concerning the birth, life, death, and resurrection of Jesus Christ were complete and were widely used in Greek and Hebrew more than 200 years prior to their fulfillment, and long before the writing of the 27 books of the New Testament.

## Old Testament Prophets

Old Testament prophets were not clairvoyant "fortune-tellers" or seers of the future in the same way that the world understands them. God's prophets were not foretelling the future. Their messages were not "predictions". They were communicating God's definite plan of redemption.

The difference is not just an issue of semantics. A "fortune teller" claims to tell us what will happen but has no power to make it come true. God's message through his prophets is a promise of what He will do. And He has the power to fulfill those promises.

People recognize the names of Nostradamus, Sylvia Browne, Edgar Cayce and others who claim the psychic ability to see into the future. There are also false prophets who have led their people into spiritual darkness – like Muhammed, Joseph Smith, Mary Baker Eddy, and Jim Jones.

## Persecution (11)

Jesus warns us against following the messages of false prophets as we approach the end of the age:

> "the disciples came to him privately, saying, "Tell us, when will these things be, and what will be the sign of your coming and of the end of the age?" And Jesus answered them, "See that no one leads you astray. For many will come in my name, saying, 'I am the Christ,' and they will lead many astray"
> **Matthew 24:3-4**

How can we know?

- **A true prophet will never contradict the revealed Word of God**:

> "If a prophet or a dreamer of dreams arises among you and gives you a sign or a wonder, and the sign or wonder that he tells you comes to pass, and if he says, 'Let us go after other gods,' which you have not known, 'and let us serve them,' you shall not listen to the words of that prophet or that dreamer of dreams. For the Lord your God is testing you, to know whether you love the Lord your God with all your heart and with all your soul.
> **Deuteronomy 13:1-3**

- **Prophecies from God are always in harmony with the whole counsel of the Lord:**

> "And when they say to you, 'Inquire of the mediums and the necromancers who chirp and mutter,' should not a people inquire of their God? Should they inquire of the dead on behalf of the living? To the teaching and to the testimony! If they will not speak according to this word, it is because they have no dawn"
> **Isaiah 8:19-20**

- **For a true prophet there is no room for error. His prophecies will always be fulfilled:**

"And if you say in your heart, 'How may we know the word that the Lord has not spoken?'— when a prophet speaks in the name of the Lord, if the word does not come to pass or come true, that is a word that the Lord has not spoken; the prophet has spoken it presumptuously. You need not be afraid of him"
**Deuteronomy 18:21-22**

- **A true Prophet will bear good fruit:**

"Beware of false prophets, who come to you in sheep's clothing but inwardly are ravenous wolves. You will recognize them by their fruits. Are grapes gathered from thornbushes, or figs from thistles? So, every healthy tree bears good fruit, but the diseased tree bears bad fruit. A healthy tree cannot bear bad fruit, nor can a diseased tree bear good fruit. Every tree that does not bear good fruit is cut down and thrown into the fire. Thus you will recognize them by their fruits."
**Matthew 7:15-20**

Old Testament Prophets were not psychic fortune telling "predictors" of the future. God spoke to and through them in order to **reveal his definite plan** – his plan, for his glory, for the encouragement and edification of his elect, and as a warning to the rest of the world.

> All of their messages pointed to their need for a Savior / Redeemer and revealed God's promise to fulfill that same need.

Persecution (11)

## **The Setting (11.2)**

When Judah was under siege at the hands of Assyria, Ahaz, King of Judah expressed his fears to Isaiah:

> [10] Again the LORD spoke to Ahaz, [11] "Ask a sign of the LORD your God; let it be deep as Sheol or high as heaven." [12] But Ahaz said, "I will not ask, and I will not put the LORD to the test." [13] And he said, "Hear then, O house of David! Is it too little for you to weary men, that you weary my God also? [14] Therefore the Lord himself will give you a sign. Behold, the virgin shall conceive and bear a son, and **shall call his name Immanuel.** [15] He shall eat curds and honey when he knows how to refuse the evil and choose the good. [16] For before the boy knows how to refuse the evil and choose the good, the land whose two kings you dread will be deserted. [17] The LORD will bring upon you and upon your people and upon your father's house such days as have not come since the day that Ephraim departed from Judah—the king of Assyria"
>
> **Isaiah 7:10-17**

Notice the offer in verse 10-11 and the response of Ahaz in the succeeding verse:

What is the promise in verse 14? _____

What is foretold concerning the enemies of Ahaz? _____

"Immanuel" is translated "God with us".
The book of **Isaiah** was written approximately 700 years before the birth of Jesus.

Warrior 141

Allied Powers

## Plan of God (11.3)

In Genesis 3, God promised an offspring of the woman that would bruise the head of the Serpent. In Genesis 15, God promised Abraham a seed that would out-number the stars in the sky. We learn from Galatians 3:15, that Christ is the fulfillment of that promise:

> "Now the promises were made to Abraham and to his offspring. It does not say, 'And to offsprings,' referring to many, but referring to one, "And to your offspring," who is Christ."
> **Galatians 3:16**

Mary and Joseph were not living in Bethlehem. God used a decree from Caesar to compel them to travel from Nazareth to Bethlehem.

> "O Bethlehem Ephrathah, who are too little to be among the clans of Judah, from you shall come forth for me one who is to be ruler in Israel, whose coming forth is from of old, from ancient days"
> **Micah 5:1-4**

**Jeremiah 31:15** foretold of a time when the children of Israel would be slaughtered. That a prophecy was fulfilled by Herod in **Matthew 2:18**.

**Hosea 11:1-2** tells us that God would call his son out of Egypt. Matthew 2:15 tells us that Mary and Joseph fled to Egypt and would not return until after Herod's death.

What do these and other prophecies tell us about the purpose and plan of God?

_____
_____
_____

Persecution (11)

## **The Promise (11.4)**

The prophet Isaiah wrote during a time (740-700 BC) when Judah was in decline and would soon fall into captivity at the hands of the Assyrians.

> "Because this people has refused the waters of Shiloah that flow gently, and rejoice over Rezin and the son of Remaliah, therefore, behold, the Lord is bringing up against them the waters of the River, mighty and many, the king of Assyria and all his glory"
>
> **Isaiah 8:6-7**

With this message of discipline, God also delivered a message of hope:

> [14] And he will become a sanctuary and a stone of offense and a rock of stumbling to both houses of Israel, a trap and a snare to the inhabitants of Jerusalem. [15] And many shall stumble on it." –
>
> **Isaiah 8:14-15**

Consider these passages:

**Isaiah 28:14-18**

**1 Peter 2:4-8**

**Romans 9:31-33**

| Allied Powers

What is the promise of this Cornerstone, and why does he call Christ a "stone of stumbling"?

_____

_____

_____

The prophecy in **Isaiah 8** tells us that Jesus Christ will be a sanctuary for his followers. But He would become a stumbling stone for many who lost sight of the purpose of the Law. Israel was so busy being "religious" by the standards of the Pharisees that they missed the fulfillment of the very Law they were called to protect.

It is easy to get caught up in "doing" the Christian life, with activities that look Christ-like and still lose sight of the essential call to exalt Christ.

> "...the original prophecy in Isaiah serves to show us that God's real objective in laying Christ in Zion was not that men might stumble at Him, but that He might be a foundation for their hopes. The real objective of God was that Christ might be the cornerstone of human confidence; but the result has been that to one set of men, renewed by almighty grace, Christ has become a sanctuary of refuge and a stone of dependence; and to others, left to their own depravity, He has become a rock of offense and a stumbling stone"
> **Charles Spurgeon** [65]

---

[65] Spurgeon, Charles, Sermon #571, Metropolitan Tabernacle, May 22, 1864, www.spurgeongems.org

Persecution (11)

## **Promise Fulfilled (11.5)**

Isaiah 9 begins with the promise:
> "there will be no gloom for her who was in anguish…in the latter time he has made glorious the way of the sea, the land beyond the Jordan, Galilee of the nations"
>
> **Isaiah 9:1**

> "And leaving Nazareth he went and lived in Capernaum by the sea, in the territory of Zebulun and Naphtali, 14 so that what was spoken by the prophet Isaiah might be fulfilled"
>
> **Matthew 4:13-14**

**Isaiah 9:2** begins with the phrase: "the people who walked in darkness have seen a great light"; leading to the familiar prophecy in Isaiah 9:6-7

Reflect on **Isaiah 9:6-7**, in light of Matthew 4 (above)

_____

_____

What does the fulfillment of this prophecy reveal about the character of God?

_____

As you reflect on God's answer to Judah's disobedience, how does that apply to us today?

_____

_____

Warrior 145

| Allied Powers

## Special Orders (11.6)

The prophet Isaiah, writing more than 700 years before the birth of Jesus:

> "Therefore the Lord himself will give you a sign. Behold, the virgin shall conceive and bear a son, and shall call his name Immanuel."
>
> **Isaiah 7:14**

**Matthew 1:18-23** tells us that an angel of the Lord appeared to Joseph, revealing to him that Mary would bear a Son, conceived by the Holy Spirit. "…and you shall call his name Jesus, for he will save his people from their sins".

The name "Immanuel" is translated "God with us".

> "Behind the second curtain was a second section called the Most Holy Place... 7 but into the second only the high priest goes, and he but once a year, and not without taking blood, which he offers for himself and for the unintentional sins of the people. 8 By this the Holy Spirit indicates that the way into the holy places is not yet opened as long as the first section is still standing"
>
> **Hebrews 9:3-9**

Scripture tells us that only the High Priest could enter the Holy of Holies once a year and then only with a sacrifice of blood. But, when Christ gave his own blood on the Cross, the veil that separated us from God's presence was torn from top to bottom and we enjoy access to an intimate relationship with God that was not available to Old Testament saints.

> "But when Christ appeared as a high priest of the good things that have come, then through the greater and more perfect tent (not made with hands, that is, not of this creation) 12 he entered once for all into the holy places, not by means of the blood of goats and calves but by means of his own blood, thus securing an eternal redemption."
>
> **Hebrews 9:11-12**

## Persecution (11)

"Is not this a strange thing that this grosser part of creation, this meaner part, this dust of it, should, nevertheless, be taken into union with that pure, marvelous, incomprehensible, divine being of whom we know so little, and can comprehend nothing at all? Oh, the condescension of it! I leave it to the meditations of your quiet moments. Dwell on it with care. **I am persuaded that no man has any idea how wonderful a stoop it was for God thus to dwell in human flesh** and to be, 'God with us'."

**Charles Spurgeon**

"In the beginning as the Word, and the Word as with God, and the Word was God. He was in the beginning with God. All things were made through him and without him was not anything made that was made"

**John 1:1-3**

"God with us." Then, if Jesus Christ is "God with us," let us come to God without any question or hesitancy. Whoever you may be, you need no priest or intercessor to introduce you to God, for God has introduced Himself to you. Are you children? Then come to God in the child Jesus who slept in Bethlehem's manger. Oh, you grey heads, you need not keep back, but like Simeon come and take Him in your arms and say, "Lord, now let Your servant depart in peace according to Your word, for my eyes have seen Your salvation." God sends an Ambassador who inspires no fear—not with helmet and coat of mail, bearing lance, does heaven's herald approach us—but the white flag is held in the hand of a child, in the hand of one chosen out of the people—in the hand of one who died, in the hand of one who, though He sits in glory, still wears the nail-prints. O man, God comes to you as one like yourself. Do not be afraid to come to the gentle Jesus. Do not imagine that you need to be prepared for an audience with Him, or that you need the intercession of a saint, or the intervention of priest or minister. Anyone could have come to the babe in Bethlehem"

**Charles Spurgeon**[66]

---

[66] Spurgeon, Charles H., "God with Us", Metropolitan Tabernacle, 26 December 1875

| Allied Powers

Immanuel, 'God with us', is an undeniable declaration of Jesus' deity. He did not come to Earth as a great teacher, prophet or philosopher. John makes it clear that Jesus was the incarnate deity spoken of by Charles Wesley in his hymn "Hark the Herald Angels Sing":

> "Veiled in flesh he Godhead see
> Hail the incarnate deity
> Pleased as man with men to dwell
> Jesus our Emmanuel" [67]

**John 1:9-11** tells us that Jesus was the true light; giving light to the entire world. Yet the world, made by his hands would not receive him.

> "And the Word became flesh and dwelt among us
> and we have seen his glory"
> **John 1 :14**

Reflect on the power of John's words. Jesus, the living Word, creator of all things, left his place beside the Father, came down from his Holy dwelling place and became

**Immanuel, "God with Us"**

As you reflect on these words, has Jesus become a casual acquaintance, a political ideology, or a cultural tradition or have you truly embraced the incredible gift of Immanuel,

"God with us"?

---

[67] Wesley, Charles, "Hark the Herald Angels Sing" 1739, Public Domain

# Suicide in April (12)

## Headline Story – Washington Post

**1 May 1945** -10:20 pm (Excerpt Washington Post ) [68]
"... came the voice of Grand-Admiral Karl Donitz, Commander-in-chief for the north of Germany. In somber tones, he announced the death of Hitler and his own succession as Fuhrer of the Reich. **Hitler had fallen "this afternoon," he said, fighting "at the head of his troops"**.

"This statement was believed by many ... But it was untrue. Hitler, as the world was later told, had died the previous day and had not fallen in action, as a heroic martyr, but had committed suicide without leaving the Bunker under the Reich chancellery where he had been since 16 January 1945."

In the early morning hours of 29 April 1945, Adolf Hitler married his long-time mistress, Eva Braun and prepared to take his own life in order to avoid the disgrace of his own defeat. The following is an excerpt of his last will and political testament: [69]

---

[68] Ada Petrova, Peter Watson – The Death of Hitler, The Full Story with New Evidence from Secret Russian Archives - 1995

[69] Axis Criminality, Nazi Conspiracy and Aggression, Government Printing Office, Washington, 1946-1948, vol. VI, pg. 259-260

# Allied Powers

"As I did not consider that I could take responsibility, during the years of struggle, of contracting a marriage, I have now decided, before the closing of my earthly career, to take as my wife that girl who, after many years of faithful friendship, entered, of her own free will, the practically besieged town in order to share her destiny with me. At her own desire she goes as my wife with me into death. It will compensate us for what we both lost through my work in the service of my people.

"What I possess belongs - in so far as it has any value - to the Party. Should this no longer exist, to the State; should the State also be destroyed, no further decision of mine is necessary.

"My pictures, in the collections which I have bought in the course of years, have never been collected for private purposes, but only for the extension of a gallery in my home town of Linz on Danube...

"I nominate as my Executor my most faithful Party comrade, Martin Bormann. He is given full legal authority to make all decisions. He is permitted to take out everything that has a sentimental value or is necessary for the maintenance of a modest simple life, for my brothers and sisters, also above all for the mother of my wife and my faithful co-workers who are well known to him, principally my old Secretaries Frau Winter etc. who have for many years aided me by their work.

"I myself and my wife - in order to escape the disgrace of deposition or capitulation - choose death. It is our wish to be burnt immediately on the spot where I have carried out the greatest part of my daily work in the course of a twelve years' service to my people."[70]

---

[70] Nazi Conspiracy and Aggression, Government Printing Office, Washington, D.C. 1946-1948 Vol. VI, Pages 259-260

## Suicide in April (12)

The document was signed by Adolf Hitler at 4:00 a.m. and witnessed by Joseph Goebbels, Martin Bormann and Colonel Nicholaus von Below

The document also included his "political testament" wherein he makes no apology for his actions. Instead, he went to great detail defending his actions and doubling down on his hatred for the Jewish race.

His final words put an exclamation point on his narcissism and self-aggrandizement shortly before he took his life and the lives of his new wife Eva and Blondi, his German Shepherd:

- "In these three decades, only love for my people and loyalty to my people have guided me in all my thoughts, actions, and life…"

- "Centuries may pass, but out of the ruins of our cities and monuments of art there will arise anew the hatred for the people who alone are ultimately responsible: International Jewry and its helpers! …"

- "The truly guilty party in this murderous struggle would also have to be held to account: the Jews!

- "After six years of struggle, which in spite of all reverses will go down in history as the most glorious and most courageous manifestation of a people's will to live…"

- "I do not want to fall into the hands of enemies who for the delectation of the hate-riddled masses require a new spectacle promoted by the Jews."

- "I die with a joyful heart in the awareness the immeasurable deeds and achievements of our soldiers at the front, of our women at home, the achievements of our peasants and workers, and the contribution, unique in history, of our youth, which bears my name."

## Allied Powers

- "From the sacrifices of our soldiers and from my own comradeship with them, there will come in one way or another into German history the seed of a brilliant renaissance of the National Socialist movement..."

- "Many very brave men and women have resolved to link their lives to mine to the very end... I too, as founder and creator of this movement, have preferred death to cowardly flight or even capitulation."

### V-E Day

The war in Europe officially began with the British declaration of war with Germany upon its invasion of Poland in 1939. In truth the war began years earlier when Adolf Hitler rose to power in Germany.

The most celebrated turning point of the war came with the D-day invasion (6 June 1944) at Normandy. From that point forward, allied forces moved toward the liberation of Paris in August, 1944.

In December 1944, Germany began what was called the "Ardennes Counteroffensive" (also known as "The Battle of the Bulge"). While Nazi troops enjoyed short term success in the Ardennes Counteroffensive, ultimately the Luftwaffe could not counter allied air-power and the ultimate German defeat proved to be imminent.

In January 1945, Hitler took refuge in his Führerbunker, where he would remain until his death on 30 April 1945.

By March, allied forces had reached the Rhine River. The Allies crossed at the town of Remagen. It was here that the Germans had failed to blow up a railway bridge in time to stop the Americans from seizing it and using it to cross into Germany's heartland.

As German defeat became more inevitable, Adolf Hitler's orders became more irrational. Many of his most loyal military leaders began ignoring orders. Mistakes in the field became punishable by death as Hitler grew more and more desperate.

## Suicide in April (12)

Heinrich Himmler made a secret offer to the Allies for a conditional German surrender. When Hitler found out, he went into a rage and ordered Himmler shot. Himmler committed suicide after being detained by the British at a checkpoint.

Adolf Hitler and Eva Braun were married at midnight on 29 April 1945 in the Führerbunker and soon after, he dictated his last will and testament. The following day, Eva Braun killed herself with a cyanide pill and Hitler shot himself in the head with his own Walther PPK 7.65 pistol.

In accordance with Hitler's instructions, both bodies were taken up into the garden of the Reich Chancellery, doused in gasoline and burned.

After declaring Heinrich Himmler and Hermann Göring to be traitors, Hitler's appointed successor as President of the Reich was Grand Admiral Karl Dönitz, with Joseph Goebbels as Chancellor. Goebbels and his wife committed suicide 2 days later on 2 May 1945.

| Allied Powers

Seven days after Hitler's suicide, acting on orders from Dönitz, General Alfred Jodl, signed for the unconditional surrender of all German forces. While fighting would continue for a few weeks after his surrender the war in Europe came to end at 2301 hours (11:01 p.m. local time) on 8 May 1945.

**Adolf Hitler**
Born 20 April 1889
Died 30 April 1945

Suicide in April (12)

## The Power of the Cross (12.1)

Christ's victory over Satan, sin, and death came at Calvary on a Roman cross, more than 2,000 years ago. The enemy continues to wage fierce battles, but his fight is the last desperate stand of a defeated foe.

> "for still our ancient foe
> doth seek to work us woe;
> His craft and power are great
> and armed with cruel hate,
> on earth is not his equal"
> (**A Mighty Fortress**)
>
> Martin Luther

In Genesis 3, God spoke to the serpent in the Garden saying "I will put enmity between your offspring and her offspring; he shall bruise your head and you shall bruise his heel". That prophecy and promise was carried out when Jesus went to the Cross.

# Τετέλεσται

*Tetelestai ...It is finished*

We read about the crucifixion and study the "Passion". We display the cross on our bumpers and in our jewelry. It is in full display in most churches. But do we really appreciate the impact of the cross – in history, in eternity, and in our own personal lives?

| Allied Powers

## Reality of the Cross (12.2)

"When they take down that precious body and wrap it in fair white linen and in spices, and lay it in Joseph's tomb, they weep as they handle the casket in which the Deity had dwelt, for there again Satan had bruised his heel. It was not merely that God had bruised him, "though it pleased the Father to bruise him," **but the devil had let loose Herod, and Pilate, and Caiaphas, and the Jews, and the Romans, all of them his tools, upon him whom he knew to be the Christ**, so that he was bruised of the old serpent. That is all, however! It is only his heel, not his head, which is bruised! For lo, the Champion rises again; the bruise was not mortal nor continual. Though he dies, yet still so brief is the interval in which he slumbers in the tomb that his holy body hath not seen corruption, and he comes forth perfect and lovely in his manhood, rising from his grave as from a refreshing sleep after so long a day of unresting toil! Oh the triumph of that hour!"

**Charles H Spurgeon** [71]

Matthew 26 tells us an encounter with a woman who worshiped Jesus by anointing him with oil. How did the disciples respond?

**Matthew 26:6-12**

Did they completely miss the statement about her anointing Jesus for his burial?

---

[71] Spurgeon, Charles H, Sermon No. 1326 – November 26, 1876

## Suicide in April (12)

**Matthew 26:14-16**
**Matthew 26:20-25**

**Matthew 26:30-35**
**Matthew 26:40**

**Matthew 28:55-56**

**Matthew 26:69-74**

In the garden of Gethsemane, Jesus agonized in prayer while his friends slept. Peter denied him when he was confronted by a little girl. When Jesus was arrested, his friends scattered. One of his friends sold him for 30 pieces of silver. The crowds that once gathered to hear his teaching now gathered to mock him and cry out for his execution.

Look back at Spurgeon's words and reflect on what Jesus endured on the way to the Cross. As you reflect on his prayer in the garden could you see the gravity of what he was about to experience? Could you see the human side of Jesus? Could you see his determination to carry out his Father's mission?

| Allied Powers

## **Destroying the Works of Satan (12.3)**

"The reason the Son of God appeared was to destroy the works of the devil"- **1 John 3:8 (ESV)**

What does he mean destroy the "**works**" of the devil?

In the passages below,
what "works" of Satan were destroyed? _____

**Genesis 3:19** _____
**Hebrews 2:14-15** _____
**1 Corinthians 15:21-26** _____
**Isaiah 25:8** _____

_____

**Revelation 12:10-11** _____
**Colossians 2:13-15** _____
**Romans 8:1** _____

_____

**John 8:34-36** _____
**Romans 6:6-14** _____

_____

**Matthew 18:7** _____
**James 1:13-15** _____
**1 Corinthians 10:13** _____

_____

**1 John 5:18-19** _____
**Revelation 12:9** _____

**John 12:31-36** _____
**Isaiah 14:12-14** _____

_____

Suicide in April (12)

# Wrath of God Was Satisfied (12.4)

[23] for all have sinned and fall short of the glory of God, [24] and are justified by his grace as a gift, through the redemption that is in Christ Jesus, [25] whom God put forward as a propitiation by his blood, to be received by faith. This was to show God's righteousness, because in his divine forbearance he had passed over former sins" –
**Romans 3:23-25**

The word "**propitiation**" is used in Romans 3:25 in the ESV, NASB and KJV, while the NIV uses the term "sacrifice of atonement". The term is offensive to many because it means to placate or appease the "wrath of God", and that seems contradictory to those who only want to talk about the loving side of God's character, with "love" as defined by the world's standards.

How does the term "propitiate" affect your view of God?

_____

_____

_____

_____

"**He has redeemed his people. He has propitiated his wrath. He has demonstrated his justice**. Indeed, these three achievements belong together. Through the sin-bearing, substitutionary death of his Son, God has propitiated his own wrath in such a way to redeem and justify us, and at the same time demonstrate his justice. We can only marvel at the wisdom, holiness, love and mercy of God, and fall down before him in humble worship. The cross should be enough to break the hardest heart, and melt the iciest."
**John Stott** [72]

---

[72] Stott, John, *The Message of Romans*, Intervarsity Press, 1994

| Allied Powers

## Righteousness of God (12.5)

Jesus satisfied the "wrath" of God if you have grown up believing that God is loving, gracious and merciful, the word "wrath" may be troubling. If this challenges your senses, you are not alone.

Read **Romans 3:5-20**. How does this passage speak to the human condition?

_____
_____
_____

**Romans 3:21-26** uses the terms "Justified", "Gift" and "Redemption". How do these terms help define God's character of "love" in tangible terms?

_____
_____
_____
_____

God's character is immutable for all eternity. God's righteous character did not change from the Old Testament to the New. God is righteous, loving, merciful and holy. He does not lay aside one aspect of his character in order to demonstrate another. He did not lay aside justice in the name of mercy.

In act of grace, he placed the weight of sin on Jesus' perfectly righteous shoulders and imputed Jesus' perfect record on his followers.

> The ultimate act of love, justice, and mercy
> was accomplished when God poured
> out his wrath on his own Son.

Suicide in April (12)

## Special Orders (12.6)

*".. we see the symbol of the cross on necklaces and on church steeples so often that we have no concept of what it meant and accomplished"*
**Ravi Zacharias** [73]

Many in the Church today, try to avoid the topics of God's righteousness, the existence of sin and a place called Hell, as if they were somehow in opposition to a "God of love". There is no contradiction between God's righteousness and his love. The reason we struggle to understand and reconcile the two is that our own definition of "love" is shallow and is typically centered around our emotions and sentiments. God's love transcends anything we can think, feel or imagine.

God's love detonated the most powerful weapon in our spiritual war when he took his Son and put him on a Roman cross to destroy the works and tyranny of Satan. Defeating Satan is not the Believer's battle. That victory was secured when God delivered his own son as the ultimate demonstration of his love, mercy, justice, and righteousness. **Satan is already defeated!**

Through the Cross, the works of Satan have been destroyed. Because of the Cross, we are no longer under the bondage of sin, the penalty for sin, nor the power of death. While the world, and the flesh and the devil will continue to attack, their power is limited and their defeat is an absolute certainty.

> "And they compelled a passerby, Simon of Cyrene, who was coming in from the country, the father of Alexander and Rufus, to carry his cross. 22 And they brought him to the place called Golgotha (which means Place of a Skull). 23 And they offered him wine mixed with myrrh, but he did not take it. 24 And they crucified him and divided his garments among them, casting lots for them, to decide what each should take.

---

[73] Zacharias, Ravi, *Jesus Among Other Gods*, Thomas Nelson, Inc., 2000

## Allied Powers

[25] And it was the third hour when they crucified him. [26] And the inscription of the charge against him read, "The King of the Jews."

"[27] And with him they crucified two robbers, one on his right and one on his left. [29] And those who passed by derided him, wagging their heads and saying, "Aha! You who would destroy the temple and rebuild it in three days, [30] save yourself, and come down from the cross!" [31] So also the chief priests with the scribes mocked him to one another, saying, "He saved others; he cannot save himself. [32] Let the Christ, the King of Israel, come down now from the cross that we may see and believe." Those who were crucified with him also reviled him.

"And when the sixth hour had come, there was darkness over the whole land until the ninth hour. [34] And at the ninth hour Jesus cried with a loud voice, **"Eloi, Eloi, lema sabachthani**?" which means, "My God, my God, why have you forsaken me?"

"[35] And some of the bystanders hearing it said, "Behold, he is calling Elijah." [36] And someone ran and filled a sponge with sour wine, put it on a reed and gave it to him to drink, saying, "Wait, let us see whether Elijah will come to take him down." [37] And Jesus uttered a loud cry and breathed his last. [38] And the curtain of the temple was torn in two, from top to bottom.

[39] And when the centurion, who stood facing him, saw that in this way he breathed his last, he said, "Truly this man was the Son of God!" –

**Mark 15:21-39**

When his Father turned his face away from him, Jesus felt the deepest pain the universe had ever inflicted on any person. God's own Son had never experienced a single moment in all of eternity when he was not in fellowship with his Father. Yet in that one moment he became the most defiled and reviled person possible when he clothed himself in the filth that belongs to you and me –

Suicide in April (12)

but not just for us. He carried the weight of the sins of the whole world; past, present, and future.

### *And on the third day...*

God's justice, mercy, grace, and love
came together in perfect harmony in the finished work
of Christ on the Cross.

"People who discount the resurrection of Jesus tend to portray the disciples in one of two ways: either as gullible rubes with a weakness for ghost stories, or as shrewd conspirators who conceived a resurrection plot as a way to jump-start their new religion"

**Philip Yancey** [74]

In Genesis 3, the poisonous serpent brought sin, sickness, and death into this world.

**In his perfect love,
God poured out his wrath on Jesus.
Jesus took our hopeless condition
to a Roman cross,
satisfied the justice of God
and destroyed the works of Satan
once and for all.**

# Τετέλεσται

*Tetelestai ...It is finished*

---

[74] Yancey, Philip, *The Jesus I never Knew*, Zondervan, Grand Rapids, Michigan 1995

| Allied Powers

# Operation Overlord (13)

**5 June 1944**
The weather forecast was questionable at best. General Dwight David Eisenhower had to make an historic decision. Further delays in the mission would likely lead to the Germans figuring out the plan, and chances of its success would go down with each day's delay.

General Eisenhower delivered an inspirational, but solemn letter that was placed into the hands of every soldier, sailor and airman set to embark on the dangerous mission known as "Operation Overlord". The General delivered the same message by radio,

## Operation Overlord (13)

displaying the confidence and leadership skills that would serve him well in the years to come.

He reminded them of the importance of the mission in the eyes of the world. He reminded them of the enemy's own ferocity, while encouraging them to fight bravely and to accept nothing less than absolute victory. He closed the statement with a prayer seeking the blessing of Almighty God for this noble mission.

While demonstrating the outward confidence of a great leader, General Eisenhower had also written a note wherein he accepted all of the blame for the failure of that mission. That note was never needed.

**5 June 1945 - 9:45 p.m.**
The wait is over - The mission is a "go".
Under orders of General Eisenhower, Operation Overlord is underway

Under plans developed in the Spring of 1944, troops would land on the beaches of Normandy under the cover of a naval bombardment of German fortifications and with aerial support of more than 13,000 fighter planes, gliders, transport planes and paratroopers.

The American First Army was to land at Caréntan-Isigny with the Fourth Infantry Division assigned to Utah Beach and the 29th Infantry Division were scheduled to take Omaha Beach. The Canadian Third Division was sent to Juno Beach and the British 50th Division was assigned to Gold Beach.

There were 156,000 Allied troops involved in the D-Day operations, including 73,000 American troops and 83,000 Canadian and British troops. They crossed the English Channel in transports and boarded amphibious landing craft that took them onto the beaches and straight into the teeth of a powerful enemy.

A total of 6,000 ships were used to transport and support the mission. The first wave involved 60,000 men and 6,800 vehicles each at Omaha and Utah beaches. Over the next two days, another 43,500 troops and 6,000 vehicles hit the beaches at Normandy.

## Allied Powers

Similar numbers of Canadian and British troops were assigned to the other landing areas. Altogether, nearly 3 million men in 47 divisions were deployed for the invasion. 21 Divisions were American. The remainder were primarily British and Canadian, with the aid of many French, Polish, Belgian, Italian, and Czech soldiers fighting for the Allies.

Each soldier engaged in the European theatre served an important role in the victory by the Allied forces. Operation Overlord was the plan that provided the power and the strategy for initiating the march across Europe and the ultimate defeat of Adolf Hitler.

After Normandy, the Allied Forces engaged many battles and suffered many casualties – but the power for victory was delivered, in large measure, on D-Day, 6 June 1944.

**Deception at Pas de Calais**
Many felt the best location for the invasion would be at Pas de Calais. It was located at the narrowest possible point in the English Channel and afforded the easiest crossing. Located well north of Normandy, it was also the point that was most defended by the Germans.

An elaborate plan was developed to convince the Germans that the invasion would, indeed, take place at the Pas de Calais. German forces were sent to reinforce Calais, leaving Normandy more vulnerable to attack.

The deception was named "Operation Fortitude". While double agents among Nazi intelligence were planting the seeds for an attack at Pas de Calais, allied forces on the English side of the Channel were busy creating a fake build-up of Allied troops, complete with inflatable tanks, dummy landing craft, decoy lighting and airfields, and phantom armies.

Operation Fortitude included deceptive radio transmissions and diplomatic communication to draw the Nazis' attention away from Normandy. Hitler had to choose. His choice would weaken

## Operation Overlord (13)

one area at the expense of the other. Pas de Calais was the most logical point to be defended.

Operation Fortitude was successful in its mission. Hitler's choice was valuable to the success of the Normandy Landings on "D-Day"

**Normandy**

Allied Forces were effective at reducing the effectiveness of German radar through jamming, decoys, and strategic bombing of radar locations. Allied minesweepers were used to clear channels for safe passage through German minefields.

Airborne paratroopers landed in France hours before dawn and allies even used dummy parachutists to confuse the Germans. Americans landed inland from Utah beach while their British counterparts arrived just to the east of them.

As the naval force approached the beaches, allied ships and aircraft bombarded German positions along the cliffs of Normandy.

**D-Day: The turning point**

For all of its glory, Operation Overlord was risky. Casualty counts were high. Many gave their lives to set the stage for the liberation of Europe. The operation was complex and incorporated all of the strategic resources that General Eisenhower and his advisors could assemble.

Even with careful planning and direction of resources, Eisenhower knew that victory was not a forgone conclusion. General Eisenhower waited until the right circumstances and the Allied invasion of Normandy on D-Day set the stage that ultimately led to victory over Nazi Germany.

Many battles were still ahead, but Hitler was now on the defense. D-Day proved to be the turning point in the defeat of Nazi Germany in World War II.

| Allied Powers

## The Power of the Holy Spirit (13.1)

Jesus promised the Holy Spirit and instructed his followers to wait until they received His power. Then, in Acts 17, we learn that the religious leaders of Thessalonica dragged Jason and some of the brothers before the city authorities, shouting:

### "These men who have turned the world upside down have come here also"

Jesus appointed twelve men to take the world by storm and to turn it upside down. But his first battle command was to wait:

> "And behold, I am sending the promise of my Father upon you. But stay in the city until you are clothed with power from on high."
>
> **Luke 24:49**

> "And while staying with them he ordered them not to depart from Jerusalem, but to wait for the promise of the Father, which, he said, "you heard from me; for John baptized with water, but you will be baptized with the Holy Spirit not many days from now."
>
> **Acts 1:4-5**

Read these passages and note the role(s) of the Holy Spirit as shown here:

**Isaiah 42:1-5:** _____
**John 16:7-15** _____
**Romans 8:5-11** _____

_____
_____
_____

## Operation Overlord (13)

It is easy to fall into the trap of trying to do God's work for him. We rely on our powers of persuasion, well thought out "plans of action", creative techniques, and even well-designed programs to do what only God can do. Jesus did not send out his Apostles until after he empowered them through his Spirit.

The Christian faith functions only under the power of the Holy Spirit. Without him, our battle with the flesh would be lost. Spiritual battles against Satan and his demonic powers would be powerless and battles with the world and its culture would be futile.

Christ promised the gift of the Holy Spirit and when his disciples experienced His power they were transformed from a band of men held hostage by fear into warriors in Christ's army.

> [7] And after there had been much debate, Peter stood up and said to them, "Brothers, you know that in the early days God made a choice among you, that by my mouth the Gentiles should hear the word of the gospel and believe. [8] And God, who knows the heart, bore witness to them, by giving them the Holy Spirit just as he did to us, [9] and he made no distinction between us and them, having cleansed their hearts by faith. [10] Now, therefore, why are you putting God to the test by placing a yoke on the neck of the disciples that neither our fathers nor we have been able to bear? [11] But we believe that we will be saved through the grace of the Lord Jesus, just as they will."
> **Acts 15:7-11**

Allied Powers

## His Power to Transform (13.2)

> "The Holy Spirit does not rest content with a mere revelation of Christ. His objective is a reproduction of Christ in the life of the believer. With this in view, He patiently works until Christ is formed in each"
> **J Oswald Sanders** [75]

Our relationship with Christ and the Holy Spirit was not the result of our own efforts:

> "And it is God who establishes us with you in Christ, and has anointed us, [22] and who has also put his seal on us and given us his Spirit in our hearts as a guarantee"
> **2 Corinthians 1:21-22**

This should encourage us. As Believers, the same God who called and established our relationship with Christ has placed an unbreakable seal on that relationship through the Holy Spirit.

Notice that the Holy Spirit does not stop with us after he has brought us to Christ:

**Ezekiel 36:25-31** _____

_____
_____
_____
_____

As you studied this passage, did you notice the number of "action" words that Ezekiel used to describe the work of the Holy Spirit?

---

[75] Sanders, J. Oswald, *Enjoying Intimacy with God*, Moody Press, Chicago, IL 1980

## Operation Overlord (13)

In Romans, we see the phrase "live by", and Titus speaks of "washing, regeneration, and renewal. What do these passages tell us about how we are to live out the Christian life?

**Titus 3:4-7**
**Romans 8:13-16**

Without the indwelling work of the Holy Spirit, life transformation is an exercise in futility. All Christian activities (worship, prayer, service, preaching, teaching, evangelism, giving, missions, etc.) are powerless without the Holy Spirit.

**1 Corinthians 2:10 - 3:2**

**John 16:12-15**

"If you do not understand a book by a departed writer you are unable to ask him his meaning, but the Spirit, who inspired Holy Scripture, lives forever, and He delights to open the Word to those who seek His instruction."
**Charles Spurgeon**

| Allied Powers

## **Empowered Prayer (13.3)**

All of us have a "conscience" that speaks to us from the depths of our experience. While our conscience can be very positive, it is not the same as the Holy Spirit. Our consciences can be shaped and even seared by our experiences in life. It also can be influenced by the enemies of Christ.

Our consciences may deceive us but the Holy Spirit will always speak the truth. In the passages below, how is the presence of the Holy Spirit manifested in the lives of Believers?

**Romans 8:26-27** _____

_____

**1 Corinthians 2:9-15** _____

As Believers, we have been given the indwelling of the Holy Spirit. He will never leave you. However, Scripture warns us that we can (and often will) resist His voice – even in our prayers.

> "Prayer is a sincere, sensible, affectionate pouring out of the heart or soul to God, through Christ, in the strength and assistance of the Holy Spirit, for such things as God has promised, or according to His Word, for the good of the church, with submission in faith to the will of God."
> **John Bunyan**

Like anything else in life, our prayers can be a collection of self-centered wishes (or demands) with its roots firmly planted in our old flesh. It is a great and powerful gift to have the indwelling Spirit to guide our thoughts and prayers when our flesh demands its way, when the world shouts at us, and when Satan seeks to take us down the path of destruction.

Operation Overlord (13)

## **His Power to Equip (13.4)**

"Then he said to me, "This is the word of the LORD to Zerubbabel: Not by might, nor by power, but by my Spirit, says the LORD of hosts."

**Zechariah 4:6**

How many ways are we equipped and how are we to use the gifts that are given by the Holy Spirit?

**Acts 1:8**
**Acts 2:1-11**

We are right to be amazed at the gifts. We should not overlook their purpose.
See 1:8 and 2:11

**1 Corinthians:**

**12:1-13**
**12:27-31**
**13:13**
**14:12**

Believers are not equally gifted. The many gifts of the Spirit are "apportioned" among Believers as **He wills**. Because they are "gifts "and not earned on the basis of our works, talents, intellect, or abilities, we have no reason to boast in any gift, nor should we be envious of others who are gifted differently. We are simply called use our gifts for the edification (building up) of the Body of Christ.

Warrior 173 |

| Allied Powers

## Baptized by the Spirit (13.5)

Paul's first letter to Christians at Corinth started with a firm reprimand to the church because of the divisions and dissentions within the church. By the time we reach chapter 12, we should keep this central message in context.

The Apostle was not as concerned with the types of gifts, as much as he was concerned about the way Christians were abusing them in the church. After he lists some of the gifts, notice what he says in these verses:

**1 Corinthians 12:7** _____
**1 Corinthians 12:11** _____
_____
_____

What about those who would argue that they have received a "second blessing", or special "Baptism of the Holy Spirit"?

**1 Corinthians 12:13** _____
_____
_____

Scripture makes it clear that the gifts of the Spirit are apportioned by God as HE WILLS. We cannot add to them by our diligent works. **All Christians are baptized by the Spirit at the moment of conversion**. In fact, our conversion is not possible without this act of the Holy Spirit.

> "There is one body and one Spirit—just as you were called to the one hope that belongs to your call— one Lord, one faith, one baptism, one God and Father of all, who is over all and through all and in all"
> **Ephesians 4:4-6**

Warrior – Page 174

Operation Overlord (13)

## **Resisting the Spirit (13.6)**

"Today is the day of Pentecost. With the blessed Holy Spirit there is no Yesterday or Tomorrow--there is only the everlasting Now. And since He is altogether God, enjoying all the attributes of the Godhead, there is with Him no Elsewhere; He inhabits an eternal Here. His center is Everywhere; His bound is Nowhere. It is impossible to leave His presence, though it is possible to have Him withdraw the manifestation of that presence."

**A.W. Tozer** [76]

**Galatians 5:16-25**
What does he mean by "Walk in the Spirit"?

_____
_____
_____

**I Thessalonians 5:16-24**
What does it mean to "quench" the Holy Spirit?

_____
_____
_____

**Ephesians 4:26-31** - What is meant by the phrase "do not grieve the Holy Spirit"

_____
_____

> Therefore, as the Holy Spirit says,
> "Today, if you hear his voice,
> 8 do not harden your hearts as in the rebellion,
> on the day of testing in the wilderness,
> 9 where your fathers put me to the test
> and saw my works for forty years.
> **Hebrews 3:7-9**

---

[76] Tozer, A.W. – This World: Playground or Battleground, Christian Publications, 1989

| Allied Powers

## Special Orders (13.7)

Every Believer is equipped with gifts of the Holy Spirit from the moment of conversion and is called to use those gifts for the spreading of the Gospel (Acts 1 and 2), for equipping of the saints, for the edification and encouragement of other Believers (1 Corinthians), and to make us ready for the spiritual battles that lie ahead.

> "A cleanly being is the dove, and we must not strew the place which the dove frequents with filth and mire, if we do he will fly elsewhere. If we commit sin if we openly bring disgrace upon our religion, if we tempt others to go into iniquity by our evil example, it is not long before the Holy Spirit will begin to grieve. **Again, if we neglect prayer, if our closet door is cob-webbed, if we forget to read the Scriptures, if the leaves of our Bible are almost stuck together by neglect, if we never seek to do any good in the world**, if we live merely for ourselves and not to Christ, then the Holy Spirit will be grieved, for thus he saith, "They have forsaken me, they have left the fountain of waters, they have hewn unto themselves broken cisterns."
>
> **Charles Spurgeon** [77]

Notice Surgeon's encouragement. He references the neglect of our prayer life and study of the word as a path to "broken cisterns". The Spirit guides us in our study of Scripture and intercedes for us in our prayers. The best way to grieve the Spirit is to neglect his revealed word and to live a prayerless life.

The indwelling of the Spirit is **permanent** for all true followers of Christ. However, we can and often will resist the voice of the Spirit and choose to follow the world, the flesh and the devil. There are also times when the flesh is so strong that we will "quench" or "grieve" the Spirit for a period of time.

---

[77] Sermon 278 - delivered Sabbath Morning, October 9th, 1859, by C. H. Spurgeon at the Music Hall, Royal Surrey Gardens

## Operation Overlord (13)

**Hebrews 3:15** tells us:

"Today, if you hear his voice, do not harden your heart". The word "today" is critical. Today, as I am walking in the Spirit, engaged in the Word and in prayer, the Spirit is in control. Tomorrow, I might respond to another voice. That is when the Spirit's voice will say "repent and turn to me".

In **I Thessalonians 5:19**

we are warned "do not quench the Holy Spirit". The word "quench" is what we use to put out a fire. Smokey Bear calls us to douse our campfires with water, stir the coals, and repeat the process until the coals are cold to the touch and unable to be reignited. For the Christian, the Holy Spirit will never reach the point where He cannot be reignited, but we certainly have the capacity to pour water on His influence in our lives.

The Holy Spirit speaks to us and we turn a deaf ear. He speaks again and we turn up the volume for of the voices of the world, the flesh and the devil to the point where is voice is barely heard. Today, when you hear his voice, do not harden your hearts, but fan the flames and allow the Spirit to consume the enemy. This is what "walking in the Spirit" looks like on a daily basis.

As Believers, we are engaged in Spiritual warfare every day. God has gifted us with weapons that are powerful in resisting the attacks of the world, the flesh and the devil. The Holy Spirit is the third person of the Trinity. He is the greatest weapon we have in our daily battle.

**Without Him defeat is certain.**
**Through Him defeat is not possible!**

General Eisenhower kept a letter in his pocket taking responsibility for the failure of Operation Overlord – just in case. Jesus needs no such letter. The Holy Spirit needs no letter. Though there are many battles ahead our ultimate absolute victory over the world, the flesh, and Satan is secured.

# Arsenal

> "The instruments of grace
> are the personal spiritual disciplines that
> God has given us for our benefit. These include time alone
> with God every day, regular reading and study of the Bible,
> Scripture memorization, and prayer. I call these the
> personal disciplines. There are also the corporate
> disciplines of worshiping together, hearing God's Word
> taught, and participating in the sacraments."
> **Jerry Bridges** [78]

As Christians, we are often tempted to live our lives at one of two opposite extremes: "The church of the Holy Bootstraps" or the "Let go and let God Fellowship", neither of which is biblical.

In the previous section we learned that the ultimate outcome of the war with the world, the flesh and the devil has already been won as a result of Christ's finished work on the Cross.

Even with victory secured, we still wrestle, on a daily basis, in battles with the same spiritual enemies. Here again, Christ has not left us unarmed. His equipping power is available to us through ordinary weapons accessible to us on a daily basis. These we refer to as the "disciplines of grace".

---

[78] "Pursuing Holiness, an Interview with Jerry Bridges", Table Talk Magazine, December 1, 2014, Ligonier Ministries

# Joseph Goebbels (14)

Joseph Goebbels' official title was Reichsminister of Public Enlightenment and Propaganda, a position in which he served from 1933 to 1945. He was one of Hitler's most trusted and loyal followers up to and including his own suicide on the day following Hitler's death by the same means.

He had two primary missions and he did them both very well. His first mission was to present Adolf Hitler and his Nazi ideology in a positive light in order to win the people and keep them loyal to Adolf Hitler. The other mission was to convince the German people that Jews were their enemy and should be exterminated.

Goebbels had the advantage of speaking to a German people who were suffering, discontent, and looking for solutions to their problems. German morale was decimated by the terms of the Treaty of Versailles that ended World War I. They were humiliated by the rest of the world. Their economy was in ruins as a result of the financial penalties imposed by the Treaty and by the impact of a world-wide Great Depression.

Goebbels was skilled at capitalizing on this discontent by painting Adolf Hitler and the Nazi ideology as the answers to all of their

| Arsenal

problems. Hitler, himself, was skilled at seducing the people in his public speeches. Goebbels role was to influence the people through control of information – in schools, entertainment, and in the news outlets.

> "... Goebbels began formulating the strategy that fashioned the myth of Hitler as a brilliant and decisive leader. He arranged massive political gatherings at which Hitler was presented as the savior of a new Germany" [79]

### Kristallnacht
Goebbels played a leading role in instigating the violent attacks on the infamous "Kristallnacht" in November, 1938. He used the murder of a German diplomat and the German media to provoke the attacks that destroyed thousands of Jewish homes, synagogues, schools and businesses. Nearly 100 Jews were killed and thousands were taken to concentration camps.

From a propaganda perspective, Kristallnacht proved to be a setback. The attacks evoked more criticism than anti-semitism. In the aftermath, Hitler directed Goebbels to adopt a different approach that would influence the German people without the overt call for violence to Jews.

### Propaganda Films
Believing that films could serve a vital role in molding public opinion, the Nazis had established a film department in 1930. Goebbels was responsible for the release of three major propaganda films with powerful anti-semitic messages.

- Jud Süß
- Die Rothschilds
- Der ewige Jude (The Eternal Jew)

The first (Jud Süß) was more successful than the others. It was presented in the form of a story and its anti-semitic message was more subtle than the others. The film was produced as an anti-

---

[79] "Joseph Goebbels", History.com, 24 March 2010

semitic version of a 1934 film with a similar title (Jew Süss) that had presented Jews as a persecuted people.

Central character in Jud Süß was a man named Joseph Süss Oppenheimer, who was depicted in every horrible way imaginable.

The approach was simple and subtle. It presented Jud Süß as the typical Jew and characterized him as immoral, materialistic, coniving, dishonest and greedy. On one end of the spectrum Jews were characterized as cut-throat capitalists and on the other end as filthy immigrants.

Like many movies and television dramas today, that present Christians as bigoted, hateful, extremists, Goebbels used the subtle approach of protraying Jews as the perpetrators of evil against other characters who are presented as innocent victims.

**Die Rothchilds**
"Die Rothchilds" was released on 7 July 1940. The film was primarily based on the Rothschild family and their desire for political and economic control of Europe. In addition to being anti-semitic, the film was anti-British and sought to make the case that the British were polluted by Jewish inflences.

Despite the positive reception by the population, it did not achive the objective of turning people against the British. The film was taken down and re-released on 2 July 1941 under the new title of "Die Rothschilds. Aktien auf Waterloo" (The Rothschilds. Shares in Waterloo). The revised film contained a much stronger anti-British message.

**Eternal Jew**
Another of Goebbels' film projects was a so-called documentary film entitled "The Eternal Jew". Goebbels was personally involved in the production of the film, which was released in 1940.

Leading up to the production of the film, the Propaganda Ministry had already put on an art exhibit in Munich and had published a book, both under the same title.

| Arsenal

In the film camera crews were sent in to the ghettos in Warsaw, Cracow, Łódź and Lubin in order to present the Jews in their true state, "before they put on the mask of civilized Europeans". Scenes were designed to create images of the Jew as a filthy group of people on the level of parasites and rodents.

The film was a direct frontal attack on the Jewish race, their culture, and their religion. It depicted Jews as a depraved, abnormal, uncivilized and parastic people. In an essay published in a monthly propaganda publication, the anonymous author called the film "The film of a 2000-year rat migration". Quoting the narrator of the film:

> "Where rats appear, they bring ruin by destroying mankind's goods and foodstuffs. In this way, they spread disease, plague, leprosy, typhoid fever, colera, dysentery, and so on. They are cunning, cowardly and cruel and are found mostly in large packs. Among the animals, they represent the rudiment of an insidious, underground destruction – just like the Jews among human beings" [80]

Hilter prefered the brutal, direct assault that chacterized "Der Ewige Jude", but Goebbels prefered the subtle approach that turned the hearts of the audience without offending. "Der Ewige Jude" did not experience the commercial success of its predecessor. Jud Süß was succesful because it was presented in the form of a story and its anti-semitic message was secondary to the story line.

**Der Stürmer (The Attacker)**
Der Stürmer was an anti-Semitic newspaper published from 1923 through the end of World War II. Hitler viewed the paper as a useful tool in influencing the "common man on the street". The paper used sensationalism to malign the Jew. It played on scandals (real or fabricated) within the Jewish community to incite its readers.

---

[80] Smith, David L, *Less than Human: Why we demean, enslave, and exterminate others,* MacMillan, 1 March 2011

## Joseph Goebbels (14)

Though the paper was more of a "Tabloid" style than serious news, it enjoyed wide circulation, in part because of its salacious stories. Jews were regularly tied to crimes (including rape) against the German people.

**Power of Propaganda**
Political movements and ideologies have recognized and used the power of propaganda for centuries. It is most powerful when administered in small but steady doses. Instead of an outright attack, peoples' emotions, fears, and attitudes grow over time until they are completely absorbed by the intended message.

Nazi propaganda was designed to use positive images to glorify Hitler, the Aryan race, and the Nazi ideology. It was designed to appeal to the national pride of a country humiliated by the outcome of World War I. In blaming their economic woes on the "Jewish bankers and financiers", they played on peoples' fears and insecurities.

The power of propaganda lies in its **subtlety and in its repetition**. It is most effective when it saturates the information stream from multiple sources. The Nazis used anti-Semitic films, newspaper cartoons, and even children's books to arouse centuries-old prejudices against Jews while creating new stereotypes about the Jewish race.

Today, we see Satan's anti-Christian propaganda in small doses and subtle suggestions on our television screens, in our school systems and in our colleges and universities. The intellectual elite are attempting to paint Christians as irrational followers of a religion filled with myths, traditions, and legends with no basis in reality.

Goebbels was less effective in his overt acts of aggression against the Jewish people, but was very effective when he presented it in a way that touched their senses and emotions. So too with the world and Satan and their influence over the flesh.

| Arsenal

## "God Breathed" (14.1)

"But as for you, continue in what you have learned and have firmly believed, knowing from whom you learned it and how from childhood you have been acquainted with the sacred writings which are able to make you wise for salvation through faith in Christ, Jesus. All Scripture is breathed out by God and is profitable for teaching, for reproof, for correction, and for training in righteousness, that the man of God may be competent, equipped for every good work"

**2 Timothy 3:14-17**

The Bible is the best-selling book in all of history. It has also been the most analyzed, critiqued and attacked book in all of history. You have probably seen some of the television "documentaries" that feature opinions from so-called "religious scholars" and others that claim to know more about biblical events than the eye-witness authors who originally wrote about them.

Read **2 Timothy 3:14-17** (above).
What does this passage say about the source of Scripture?

_____
_____
_____
_____
_____

As a practical matter, we are living in an age where the average Christian has almost given up on the regular reading of Scripture and replaced it with the "verse-of-the-day" postings on social media and internet blogs.

When we, as Christians, neglect the regular reading, study, and meditation on God's revealed word, we can find ourselves susceptible to outside influences that distort and diminish our view of Scripture.

Joseph Goebbels (14)

## The Attacks (14.2)

One of the more popular and "well-respected" attacks on the veracity of Scripture came from the "Jesus Seminar", launched in 1985 by the Westar Institute, with the stated goal of establishing a "scholarly" consensus on the historical accuracy of the sayings and events attributed to Jesus in the gospels. During the process, a group of "scholars" are allowed to vote on whether the events and sayings actually happened. The following is an excerpt from one of those "scholars":

> "The belief that the prophets were pointing to Jesus, though perhaps helpful at the time Matthew wrote his gospel, has **long since outlived its usefulness**. It is a belief that distorts the scriptures and has had ugly consequences in history. Out of respect for Judaism and for the Bible, therefore, I propose that Christians have an intellectual and moral duty to abandon this obsolete, self-serving, and dangerous belief. What do you think?" [81]
>
> **Robert J. Miller**

In light of **1 Timothy 6:3-5,** how would you answer Miller's challenge:

_____
_____
_____

Miller is just one in a long list of people who have attacked Scripture throughout the course of history. Miller and others who pick and choose which parts of Scripture they want to believe or reject, have had to make a volitional decision to anoint themselves as ultimate "arbiters of truth", based on their own "superior knowledge" and wisdom, and overriding the eyewitness testimony of the authors who wrote under the direction of the Holy Spirit.

---

[81] Miller, Robert J – *Born Divine*, Polebridge Press, 2001

| Arsenal

## Eye Witness Answers (14.3)

"the Bible's authority is so strong, so supreme that it imposes on us a moral obligation to believe it"
**R.C. Sproul** [82]

What do the following passages say to us concerning the authority, motivation, and the power of Scripture?

**1 Timothy 6:1-5** ———————————————————
**2 Peter 1:15-21** ———————————————————

**Ephesians 4:11-14** ——————————————————

"We are on much firmer ground when we believe the men that were there rather than the revisionists living two thousand years after these events" [83] -
**Erwin Lutzer**

"The authority of Scripture does not depend on the testimony of any man or of the church; its authority depends and rests wholly on God, the supreme author of the Bible. Scripture should be received, not so that it can become the Word of God, but because it already is the Word of God"
**R.C. Sproul**

If we study Scripture consistently and regularly, most of us will encounter challenges to our own thought processes and even what we believe is "rational". When we find ourselves in this position, we can be led astray by our own flesh or by the words of others.

---

[82] Sproul, R.C., *Truths We Confess, A Layman's Guide to the Westminster Confession of Faith*, P&R Publishing, Phillipsburg, NJ 2006

[83] Lutzer, Erwin W., *The Da Vinci Deception*, Tyndale House Publishers, Inc. Wheaton, Ill, 2004

Joseph Goebbels (14)

## The "Scholars" (14.4)

According to Wikipedia:
> "The story of the exodus is the founding myth of Israel, telling of the Israelites deliverance from slavery by Yahweh which made them his chosen people according to the Mosaic covenant. The Book of Exodus is not a historical narrative in any modern sense: modern history writing requires the critical evaluation of sources, and **does not accept God as a cause of events**"

The Wikipedia article goes to great lengths to reinvent the origins of the book of Exodus, along with the other four books of the Pentateuch (Genesis, Leviticus, Numbers and Deuteronomy). Time and space will not permit us to address the many inconsistencies in the Wikipedia article. Suffice it to note that the central assumption to the "scholars'" approach to the Book of Exodus, the Passover, and to Scripture as a whole is revealed in the last sentence of the paragraph above:

**"Modern history does not accept God as a cause of events"**

Why do they start with an assumption that denies God? Look at Jesus' words:

**John 15:23-25**

_____

_____

_____

In verse 25, Jesus takes us back to the Old Testament – to Psalm 69:4, quoting the words of David:

> "More in number than the hairs of my head are those who hate me without cause; mighty are those who would destroy me, those who attack me with lies"

Simply put, the world hates Jesus. The world is an enemy to God, and will stop at nothing to deny His works. They point to difficult passages and, without any real investigation they pile them up as

Warrior 187 |

| Arsenal

their "evidence". The real issue with them is that many of their alternative explanations are bizarre in and of themselves.

Norman Geisler (North American Missions Board) published an excellent article addressing the so-called scholars who would attack the veracity of the Bible. [84]

In one section of his article Geisler points to challenges in nature/science:

> "When a scientist comes upon an anomaly in nature, he does not give up further scientific exploration. Rather, the unexplained motivates further study. Scientists once could not explain meteors, eclipses, tornadoes, hurricanes, and earthquakes. Until recently, scientists did not understand how the bumblebee could fly. All of these mysteries have yielded their secrets to relentless patience. Scientists do not now know how life can grow on thermo-vents in the depths of the sea. **But no scientist throws in the towel and cries "contradiction**!"

Our approach to difficult passages in Scripture should be addressed with the same attitude. The truth of Scripture does not rest on our ability to understand or explain. Instead of rejecting what we do not understand, we must take the opportunity to learn more. There are no errors in Scripture – dig deeper!

---

[84] Geisler, Norman, "Are there any errors in the Bible", www.namb.net/apologetics/are-there-any-errors-in-the-bible

Joseph Goebbels (14)

## **New Testament Church? (14.5)**

One of the ways that Satan is making in-roads into the culture is through our own churches. Instead of defending the truth of Scripture, many churches are walking away from the discussion and wandering into dangerous complicity with the world by denying the importance and historicity of the 39 books of the Old Testament.

Jesus quoted from all five books of the Pentateuch. He quoted from the prophetic writings of Isaiah, Jeremiah, Daniel, Hosea, Jonah, Micah, Zechariah, and Malachi. There are many examples where Jesus referred to the Old Testament. Consider these examples:

**Matthew 4:4**
**Deuteronomy 8:3**

**Mark 8:17-18**
**Jeremiah 5:21**

**Luke 20:37**
**Exodus 3:1-6**

**Matthew 12:38-41**
**Jonah 1:17**

Jesus referred to Noah and the Flood in Luke 17 and immediately follows with a reference to Lot. In Luke 11, he referred to the murder of Abel. If Jesus really is who he says he is (the Second person of the Trinity), surely his words carry more weight than those of the critics and revisionists living 4,000 years after the fact.

| Arsenal

After his resurrection, Jesus is seen walking and talking with two men near a village called Emmaus. Not recognizing him, these men told Jesus of the events of his crucifixion and how they had hoped he would be the one to redeem Israel.

Note Jesus' response to these men on the Emmaus road:

**Luke 24:27-32**
_____

_____
_____

Jesus identified himself through Moses (the Pentateuch) and the prophets.

If you are tempted to believe the internet postings or the words of modern-day "scholars", or the television "documentaries" that continue to deny the miracles of Christ, the supernatural acts of God and the historicity of the Scriptures – our choices are clear and simple:

- Believe the speculations of modern day "scholars" who start with denial of God and fantasize about a universe that created and sustains itself without power or cause;
- Believe the eye-witness testimonies of the human writers of Scripture who were guided by the Holy Spirit;
- Believe Jesus.

The so-called "scholars" speak as if they have the voice of authority. They speak as if they have weighed all of the possible options. But they haven't.

A true researcher or scientist does not have to start with a belief in the God of the Bible. But they have an intellectual and rational obligation to at least consider God as a "possibility". Instead, they start with a bias that actively rejects God and any possibility of His supernatural acts. As a result, they are launched into a sea of random speculations and theories that often lead them to some very bizarre conclusions for which even they have no answers.

Joseph Goebbels (14)

## **Special Orders (14.6)**

Today's culture places a high value on convenience and expediency. We are willing to pay a higher price to have our morning latte delivered rather than to have to walk to the local coffee shop or brew it ourselves. The internet, television, and social media are the all-encompassing sources of information for many in our society. They are quick, easy and efficient.

This attitude comes with a cost when it comes to Bible study and meditation. It is far easier to read a "verse of the day" or an inspirational quote than it is to open the book and read the Bible in context. Reading a verse out of context is dangerous in and of itself. But that danger is magnified many times over when we see, read, or hear alternate versions of Scripture on television specials, internet blogs, or even from the pulpits of churches where the pastor/teacher has altered or watered-down the message of Scripture.

Hitler used his Minster of Enlightenment and Propaganda to seduce and deceive the people of Germany and its neighboring countries. He controlled the media. He controlled the entertainment industry. He controlled the message of the school systems. He censored all opposition to Hitler's ideology.

Satan has a great amount of power in influencing this world. He, like Joseph Goebbels, knows that there is great power in deception and propaganda. Alter the truth, but do it in a way that is pleasing to the people and you will own them. The world and Satan have a plan for spoon-feeding their message to people who do not want to take the effort to read, meditate, and search the Scriptures.

Repeating what we said about Goebbels:
**"The power of propaganda lies in its subtlety and in its repetition".** The antidote to this propaganda is a heavy dose of the truth. A daily habit of reading, studying, and meditating on Scripture will go a long way in turning off the noise of the world and its version of the truth.

| Arsenal

## The "Scholars"

In our culture today, Wikipedia, Google, Snopes, and a few others have become the "authoritative arbiters of truth". Wikipedia and Snopes go to great lengths to footnote their sources in order to impress us with their "research". The underpinning of these and many other sites is an aversion to Scripture and a rejection of God. The numbers of their "sources" are not as important as the truth (or lack thereof) of each one of their sources. They claim to be "fact checkers", but most of their "facts" are irresponsible speculations about what would, could, or might have happened.

The "scholars" start with a denial of the only plausible explanation for the events in the Old and New Testaments. That's like trying to explain a tree branch on the ground by starting with a denial of gravity! Without a supernatural force that transcends all of the known "natural laws" of physics and other sciences, there is no explanation of the origins of the Universe nor the origins of life in the Universe.

## Supernatural Events

Matthew, Mark, Peter, John, and James all witnessed the supernatural acts of Jesus, from feeding the 5,000 to calming the storms to healing of the lame, raising the dead and Peter walking on water. These disciples were eye-witnesses to the supernatural and they were willing to be executed instead of recanting their own stories.

To start the conversation by denying the possible existence of a supernatural force is problematic in and of itself.

After demonstrating his own supernatural powers, Jesus went on to affirm the events of the Old Testament, using them as teaching tools for his ministry. Then he walked out of a grave on Easter Sunday, an act for which the critics have no plausible explanation.

Peter walked on water ("scholars" say it might have been a "sand-bar"). So they are suggesting that Peter, a life-long professional fisherman could not tell if he was standing on water or a sand bar? The "scholars" stake a claim to rational thought?

### The "New Testament Church"

More and more Pastors are presenting a message that dilutes or minimizes the teaching of the Old Testament. They do this to placate the world and fill their pews and offering plates. The world would prefer a softer lesson. The people who put Jesus on the cross did not like his message either. Jesus regularly quoted from and/or referred to the Old Testament. He regularly told the crowd and the religious leaders of his day that He was the fulfillment of the Old Testament.

For those of you with a "red-letter" Bible, you might take notice of how often those red-letters (words of Jesus) contain quotes or references to the Old Testament. He clearly placed an importance on the teachings of the Old Testament and so should we.

### "God Breathed"

The Bible is the most amazing document in all of history. It was written by 40 different human authors over the course of 1,500 years, on three (3) continents, and in three (3) different languages. Yet it is not a collection of 66 different books. All of these variables are presented without error or contradiction and present one unified message of redemption through Jesus Christ. That message has withstood more "critical analysis" than any other book in history.

### The "scholars" attack the Bible, because they fear its power.

The power of propaganda lies in its **subtlety and in its repetition.** The antidote to these false messengers is a heavy dose of the truth. We fall prey to Satan's propaganda campaign because we have developed a lifestyle that has reduced Scripture to a jar full of inspirational quotes. We have a growing need for a heavy dose of the Truth in our daily lives.

| Arsenal

# Dimples 82 (15)

*"I don't defend Scripture any more
than I would defend a lion.
I just open the cage and let him loose"*
Charles Spurgeon

**6 August 1945**

The mission designated "Dimples 82" originated on 6 August 1945 from the tiny island of Tinian. The aircraft was a Boeing B-29 "Superfortress" nicknamed the "Enola Gay" – named for the mother of Colonel Paul Tibbets, pilot of the mission.

Of the twelve crewmembers on board, only Colonel Tibbets knew the exact nature of the mission. Colonel Tibbets was 29 years old at the time of the mission. Chosen months earlier, he was the one who selected the other 11 crewmembers. Because of the risks, Colonel Tibbets also carried 12 cyanide tablets with him on the mission, to be used in the event of their capture.

The Enola Gay departed runway Able at 2:45 am on 6 August 1945. **Flight destination – Hiroshima**. She would be escorted by two other B-29s, "The Great Artiste" and "Necessary Evil" which carried scientific observers, photographic equipment and blast measurement instrumentation. Leaving Tinian, the Enola Gay met her two escorts over Mount Suribachi (Iwo Jima). They maintained a flight altitude of 9,300 feet until they were within an hour of their destination.

# Dimples 82 (15)

## "Little Boy"

Enola Gay's payload consisted of a 9,700-pound atomic device loaded in the forward bomb bay compartment of the plane. "Little Boy" was coated with dull gunmetal paint and decorated with handwritten messages to Japanese Emperor Hirohito.

As Enola Gay passed over Saipan, former Naval gunnery officer William "Deek" Parsons moved into position to arm "Little Boy" for its rendezvous with history. Parsons had been pulled from sea duty in 1943 to work on the Manhattan Project [85].

## Hiroshima

The Enola Gay climbed to 30,700 feet as she got within one hour of her target.

Bombardier Major Thomas Ferebee took his position. The entire crew donned goggles with polarized lenses to protect them from a flash expected to be 10 times the intensity of the sun. Major Ferebee located his target, the Aioi Bridge", opened the bomb bay doors, announced "bomb away" and released "Little Boy" on its six-mile freefall into history.

"Little Boy" would take 83 seconds to reach his detonation altitude of 1,890 feet. Following its release, Colonel Tibbets turned

---

[85] The Manhattan Project was the U.S. Government research project that ultimately developed the atomic bomb.

| Arsenal

the Enola Gay into a 60 degree banked turn that gave tail gunner George R. (Bob) Caron the best view of he would later call the "Fire of a Thousand Suns".

**A Different World**
The Enola gay touched down at Tinian almost exactly 12 hours after she had departed. The same day and the same runway. But a much different world.

**Nagasaki**
9 August 1945, three days after her mission to Hiroshima, Enola Gay would serve as weather reconnaissance aircraft for another B-29. This one was named "Bockscar", whose mission would deliver another atomic device named "Fat Man" to Nagasaki.

## You may not know

Two "atomic bombs" were deployed in August, 1945, but they were entirely different types of weapons in terms of their composition and explosive power.

The first bomb, "Little Boy" used at Hiroshima:
- Had a Uranium core, roughly the size of a softball;
- Its explosive power was roughly the equivalent of 15,000 tons of TNT
- "Little Boy" weighed in at 9,700 lbs.

You may or may not be aware that less than 2% of "Little Boy's" Uranium actually detonated over Hiroshima. This deadly weapon was so "inefficient" that 98% of its fissile material never underwent the chain reaction that was intended.

The second bomb, "Fat Man", was used at Nagasaki, and was 10 times more efficient than the first:
- "Fat Man" had a Plutonium core, roughly the size of a tennis ball.
- Its explosive power was roughly equivalent to 21,000 tons of TNT
- Total weight 10,800 lbs.

Both weapons were approximately 10 feet long, but "Fat Man" was twice the diameter of "Little Boy" (60 inches vs. 28 inches".

Their triggering mechanisms were completely different.

**"Little Boy"** utilized a gun-type where an explosive device fires causing one portion of the Uranium to collide with the second portion, and a fission reaction is the result.

**"Fat Man"** utilized an "implosion mechanism". Explosives surrounded the Plutonium Core, and a shock wave initiated the fission reaction.

They were two distinctly different weapons with similar powerful results.

| Arsenal

## Tinian

Both missions originated on the tiny island of Tinian, located approximately 1,500 miles south of Japan. The island was captured in the summer of 1944. Navy construction battalions known as the SeaBees began bulldozing mere days after the island was secured. Six runways were completed within two months and Tinian soon became the biggest air base in the world.

> "Tinian is a miracle. Here, 6,000 miles from San Francisco, the United States armed forces have built the largest airport in the world. A great coral ridge was half-leveled to fill a rough plain, and to build six runways, each an excellent 10-lane highway, each almost two miles long. Beside these runways, stood in long rows the great silvery airplanes. They were not by the dozen, but by the hundred. **From the air this island, smaller than Manhattan, looked like a giant aircraft carrier**"-
> 
> Phillip Morrison [86]

## Unimaginable Power

Historians will continue to debate the necessity and morality of what was done at Hiroshima and Nagasaki. Some have argued that there is no justification for ever using this type of device. Others will argue that President Truman made the right decision under the circumstances.

Two facts remain for which there is no debate. First, there is no debate about the incredible power of the device that was released from the Enola Gay on that historic day. Second, the entire world was changed so that, even after seventy (70) years, the world has managed to avoid a repeat of this destructive event.

---

[86] Richard Rhodes, *The Making of the Atomic Bombs*, Simon and Schuster, New York 1986

## Dimples 82 (15)

The power of "Little Boy" was concealed inside an enclosure roughly 10 feet long by 28 inches. Bombardier Thomas Ferebee did not create the explosion that led to the end of the war. He merely opened the bomb bay doors and released the powerful device. He had no control over the events that happened next.

Ferebee's job was simply to open<br>
the bomb bay doors and release "Little Boy"<br>
to do its work.

## Unleashing the Power

"The Word of God is like a lion. You don't have to defend a lion. All you have to do is let the lion loose, and the lion will defend itself."
**Charles H Spurgeon**

| Arsenal

## "Profitable" (15.1)

"But as for you, continue in what you have learned and have firmly believed, knowing from whom you learned it and how from childhood you have been acquainted with the sacred writings which are able to make you wise for salvation through faith in Christ, Jesus. All Scripture is breathed out by God and is profitable for teaching, for reproof, for correction, and for training in righteousness, that the man of God may be competent, equipped for every good work"

**2 Timothy 3:14-17**

As a practical matter, we are living in an age where the average Christian has almost given up on the regular reading of Scripture and replaced it with the "verse-of-the-day" postings on social media and internet blogs.

Scripture is being treated as a collection of inspirational "one-liners" posted on bumper stickers, signs, social media, and even on tattoos.

Look back at **2 Timothy 3:14-17**. What does this passage say about the power of Scripture?

_____
_____
_____

Paul encouraged Timothy to continue in what he had learned from his childhood. What "sacred writings" (verse 14) could Paul be referring to?

_____
_____
_____
_____

## Dimples 82 (15)

Many mainline churches today are minimizing the message of the Old Testament and some are even presenting it as irrelevant and unimportant. Paul (in the New Testament) seems to have a completely different message for Timothy.

Read **2 Timothy 4:1-5**
What are the warnings in this passage?

_____

_____

_____

Satan's first assault on the Word of God came in the Garden of Eden when he posed the question "Did God really say". His assaults have continued throughout history and will continue through the agency of the world and its culture until the day he is cast into the fires of Hell.

He attacks, not because he disbelieves the Bible, but because he is aware of and fears its power it has on and over the lives of men and women under its influence.

Spurgeon's words are important. To unleash the power of Scripture – we simply have to open the cage of the lion and let him do his work –

**and the Lion speaks from all 66 books
from Genesis 1 to Revelation 22.**

.

| Arsenal

## "Authority of the Word" (15.2)

Before you decide what or who to believe you must, of necessity, accept or reject Jesus' statement in **Matthew 5:18**:

> "For truly I say to you, until heaven and earth pass away, not an iota, not a dot, will pass away from the law until all is accomplished".

Like the propaganda of Joseph Goebbels, Christians today are being fed a steady stream of misinformation that is not only influencing the Christian, but is also making its way into the pulpit. The question we have to answer is whether we will believe the words of Jesus – or the words of the revisionists who came 2,000 years later.

According to Wikipedia:
> "The Exodus is the founding myth of Israel, telling how the Israelites were delivered from slavery by their god Yahweh and therefore belong to him through the Mosaic covenant"

Robert Funk (Jesus Seminar)
> "scholars theorize that the New Testament gospels were composed during the last quarter of the first century by third-generation authors on the basis of folk memories preserved in stories that had circulated by word of mouth for decades"
> **Robert Funk** [87]

> "Exodus was created by priests in Jerusalem who used a series of old legends and distorted memories which had no relationship to history" –
> **Rabbi Sherwin Wine**

---

[87] Funk, Robert, *The Five Gospels: What Did Jesus really Say*, (New York: Scribner, 1993)

## Dimples 82 (15)

Over time, the "Jesus Seminar" eventually concluded that 84% of the Gospel accounts are inaccurate, yet Jesus said not a "jot or tittle", not an "iota or dot" would pass away.

More recently, in 2003 Dan Brown's fictional novel "DaVinci Code" took the world by storm. Even though Mr. Brown admits that the book and the movie are fictional, the book was translated into 44 languages and sold more than 80 million copies.

The book created a fantastical conspiracy theory surrounding the "Holy Grail", Jesus' sexualized relationship with Mary Magdalene and the early Church's arbitrary rejection of selected books of the Bible.

> Why is the Bible the most assailed book in history?
> Why do the world and Satan find it so urgent
> to analyze and criticize the Bible?

Many great books have been written addressing the myriad attacks on Scripture. For centuries the attacks have been presented and answered by well-respected and trustworthy authors. The first challenge came from Satan himself when he called Adam and Eve to question the word of God:

**"Did God Really Say?"**

It is our objective to insure that we, as followers of Christ, do not fall victim of the world's version of the Gospel and the version of the Bible **as edited by Satan himself**:

Read **Hebrews 4:12-13**

_____
_____
_____

| Arsenal

> "If you take away the
> authority of the Word,
> you're launched on a sea
> of moral relativism with no rudder.
> We must all submit to God's Word,
> no matter how difficult or costly."
> **Steven Cole** [88]

With the myriad of attacks, few of us are equipped to answer each and every one. Those of us who are curious enough will find the time and resources to address the ones that make us uncomfortable. Suffice it to say that all of the attacks have a common thread. Most are regurgitations and restated versions of older attacks that have already been answered.

But the attacks will continue until Christ returns. Our best answer is the one Jesus used against Satan in the wilderness:

**Matthew 4:1-11**

_____

_____

_____

> "The Bible cannot err, since it is God's Word, and God cannot err. This does not mean there are no difficulties in the Bible. But the difficulties are not due to God's perfect revelation, but to our imperfect understanding of it. **The history of Bible criticism reveals that the Bible has no errors, but the critics do.**"
>
> **Norman Geisler** [89]

---

[88] Cole, Stephen, *How Temptation Works*, Genesis 3:1-7, January 14, 1996

[89] Geisler, Norman, "Are there any errors in the Bible", namb.net, North American Missions Board, Atlanta, Ga.

Dimples 82 (15)

## **Appropriating the Power (15.3)**

*"I don't defend Scripture any more
than I would defend a lion.
Just open the cage and let him loose"*
**Charles Spurgeon**

Josiah started his reign as king of Judah at the age of eight (following the reign of Manasseh and Amon) In the 18th year of Josiah's reign, Hilkiah, the high priest discovered the Book of the Law.

Read **2 Kings 22** – especially verses 8-13:

_____
_____
_____
_____

Imagine the preacher from your local church standing in front of his congregation: "We were cleaning out the storage building and stumbled on an old book (Bible) our church used to read years ago".

Hilkiah was the High Priest! The king looked to the High Priest for spiritual direction. Notice the words of the king (Josiah):

> "Go, inquire of the Lord for me,
> and for the people, and for all Judah,
> concerning the words of this book that has been found. For great is the wrath of the Lord that is kindled against us, **because our fathers have not obeyed the words of this book,** to do according to all that is written concerning us."
> **2 Kings 22:13**

It is sobering to think how many of our modern day churches are functioning like Judah in the days of Josiah.... a Bible in the storehouse with an occasional verse or passage to quote!

Warrior 205 |

| Arsenal

Read **2 Kings 23** and take note of Josiah's response to the reading of Scripture:

_____

_____

_____

_____

"Just as water is the only thing that can relieve thirst in the desert, the provision of God's Word is the only thing that can satisfy our spiritual thirst. It's the only thing that can give us encouragement in times of trial and direction for our busy lives" –

**Jim George** [90]

"Have you a spiritual taste, dear Hearer?
It is one thing to hear the Word. It is another thing to taste it. Hearing the Word is often blessed, but tasting it is a more inward and spiritual thing—it is the enjoyment of the Truth in the innermost parts of our being! **Oh, that we were all as fond of the Word as were the old mystics who chewed the cud of meditation till they were fattened upon the Word of the Lord** and their souls grew strong in the Divine Love! I am sure of this—the more you know of God's Word, the more you will love it!"

**Charles Spurgeon**

---

[90] George, Jim, *A Man After God's Own Heart*, Harvest House Publishers 2002, Eugene, Oregon

Dimples 82 (15)

# Diluting the power (15.4)

"The infallible rule of interpretation of Scripture is the Scripture itself: and therefore, when there is a question about the true and full sense of any Scripture (which is not manifold, but one), it must be searched and known by other places that speak more clearly"

**Westminster Confession of Faith**

Read Acts 17:1-4: What do you think it means "He reasoned from the Scriptures?

**Acts 17:1-4**

What did Paul experience with the people at Berea?
**Acts 17:10-13**

**Acts 17:16-21**

As you read the remainder of Acts 17, you will see a pattern that takes place in Paul's ministry. At each stop, he "reasoned" from the Scriptures. There were some who engaged and "searched" the Scriptures while there were others who resisted and attacked him from the start.

In Acts 18:4, the pattern continued as he "reasoned" in the synagogue at Corinth and in Acts 18:19 he did the same at Ephesus. The same is true for Acts 19:8-9

In **Acts 19:10:**
"This continued for two years, so that all the residents of Asia heard the word of the Lord, both Jews and Greeks"

| Arsenal

Today's Bible critics have not invented anything new. They start with a denial of the truth of Scripture and cobble together a collection of passages that support their position. When you look at their "criticism" you mostly find phrases, sentences, and verses that are quoted out of context or twisted to fit their position.

The people who start with an attack on Scripture very rarely begin with an unbiased search for knowledge. For those truly searching for understanding, Paul "reasoned" with them and helped them "search" the Scriptures for understanding.

Notice Paul's choice of words. This was no casual reading of the Scriptures. They read, researched, wrestled and studied because they wanted to tap into the power of Scripture.

Another important point to consider is that Paul reasoned from the Scriptures. What Scriptures? The New Testament had not been written. Any pastor, teacher or critic who tries to minimize the importance of the Old Testament is teaching contrary to Jesus and the Apostle Paul. The Old Testament was central to both of their teaching ministries.

- We dilute the power of Scripture when we minimize the importance of any of its 66 books;
- We dilute the power of Scripture when we reduce it to a "verse of the day" fortune cookie;
- We dilute the power of Scripture when we listen to the critics without searching, reasoning, and meditating on its teaching;
- We dilute the power of Scripture when we read it out of context.

The atomic bomb was powerful. But its power would not have had its effect unless it was armed and the bomb bay doors opened. Scripture is more powerful than any atomic device

Dimples 82 (15)

## Special Orders (15.5)

If the Japanese could have prevented Robert Caron from opening the bomb bay doors of the Enola Gay, the outcome of World War II would have been much different.

For thousands of years, Satan has recognized the power of Scripture and has worked diligently to keep its pages closed. When released, the caged lion that Spurgeon spoke of has the power surpassing that of many atomic bombs.

> The world culture and Satan himself fear
> Scripture because of its power.

The world tells us that Scripture is irrelevant and outdated fantasy. Your flesh finds some parts of Scripture objectionable, creating skepticism. You struggle with difficult passages that, at least in your own mind, appear contradictory. You struggle because the flesh continues to create doubt. In practice, we are sometimes no different from the Westar Institute. We unwittingly appoint ourselves as arbiters of the truth, picking and choosing what we want to believe.

The Bible is the "God-breathed", infallible, inerrant, and authoritative Word of the living God. Once you reject it, you are left with a conglomeration of random philosophies with no authority, no truth, and no power. You become like the ship's captain who followed the same star night after night until he realized it was a lamp on the bow of his own ship.

> "I have found that the doubts that afflict me from many sources – from science, from comparative religion, from an innate defect of skepticism, from aversion to the church – take on new light when I bring those doubts to the man named Jesus"-
>
> **Philip Yancey** [91]

---

[91] Yancey, Philip, *The Jesus I never Knew*, Zondervan, Grand Rapids, Michigan 1995

| Arsenal

> "Remember that it is not hasty reading—but serious meditation on holy and heavenly truths, which makes them prove sweet and profitable to the soul. **It is not the mere touching of the flower by the bee which gathers honey—but her abiding for a time on the flower which draws out the sweet.** It is not he who reads most, but he who meditates most—who will prove to be the choicest, sweetest, wisest and strongest Christian."
>
> **Thomas Brooks**

Go back and read this again! To draw out the sweet, we need to abide in the Word – far more than a hasty reading. Read, meditate, then read and meditate again as the power of God's word transforms your life.

The power of Scripture is summed up by Jesus when tempted in the wilderness. To everything Satan threw at him the answer was simply "**It is written**" (Luke 4:8).

Game, set, and match – there is no better answer for what the world, flesh and the devil may throw at us than *"It is written"*. But if we don't know what is written, how will we answer?

Jesus was the author of the Word. He knew the difference between biblical truth and a counterfeit presentation of God's Word. Jesus knew what was written.

Josiah discovered the power of Scripture. Before he could appropriate that power, he had to find it in the storehouse, open its pages, and let it transform a nation.

Scripture has the power to pierce the heart and transform lives. For this very reason, the Enemy is continuously on the attack with television specials, false teachers, a scientific community that denies God, the educational elite and others to barrage you with the same statement Satan started with in the Garden: **"Did God really say?"**

Dimples 82 (15)

## Absolute Truth

Many books have been written with some challenging and others defending the veracity and power of Scripture. The battle will continue until Christ returns. The battle will continue because the truth of Scripture is central to the Believer's battle. The world, the flesh and the devil will never concede because they fear its power.

However, the debate is over and the critics have lost. Like Japan in World War II and like the Adversary (Satan) himself, the critics will never surrender until they meet Christ face to face (and they certainly will).

We may or may not ever be called to debate the issue with others. **But Satan will certainly call us to debate it with ourselves**. For the world, the flesh and the devil, Scripture is a weapon that is greatly feared. It has incredible power.

When the flesh calls you to doubt God, does a particular passage come to mind? When you are faced with an important decision, or a crisis in life, can you quote or paraphrase a passage to address it? Satan will take you to the desert. The world and the flesh will challenge you. How will you answer?

Jesus used Scripture against Satan with the phrase "It is written". **To appropriate the power of Scripture our own spiritual battles, we need to know what is written.** To know it, we have to read, memorize and meditate... and repeat.

## Appropriate the Power

The crew of the Enola Gay had to load the "Little Boy" and arm it for detonation at the proper altitude. Once armed and released, they let it go and watched its power, 10 times brighter than the sun - and the world was forever changed.

The writer of Hebrews tells us that the Word of God is living, active, and powerful. But that power can only be unleashed when the Book is opened.

# Arsenal

"Most believers in the United States own several printed copies of the Bible and also have the ability to read it on a myriad of electronic devices. It is both tragic and ironic, then, that multitudes of professing Christians do not read or study their Bibles consistently. Biblical literacy in the West is at its lowest point in centuries. Even among those who do read the Bible, large portions of it remain uncharted territory"

**R. C. Sproul**

When we treat the Bible as a table ornament or confine it to the bookshelf, it is no more powerful than an antique weapon sealed behind the glass in a museum. When we reduce our Bible to a "verse of the day" inspirational quote, we dilute its power to the level of a fortune cookie or horoscope.

Every verse in Scripture is written with context. Every page in the Old and New Testament is written with authority (Holy Spirit), purpose and power.

## To unleash its power, we have to "open the cage and let him loose".

## Gibraltar (16)

The famous "Rock of Gibraltar" is located on a very narrow pass (Strait of Gibraltar) leading from the Atlantic into the

Overlooking the entrance to the Mediterranean from a height of 1,398 feet

Gibraltar

Mediterranean. At its narrowest point, Europe and Africa are separated by only 8.9 miles of water. Throughout history, Gibraltar has served as a military outpost because of its strategic location which, in turn, gives its occupants power to control the entrance to and exit from the Mediterranean.

Although Gibraltar shares a border with Spain it is, in fact, a colony of the United Kingdom.

| Arsenal

### Tunnels of Gibraltar

In June, 1779, while Britain was still engaged with America's war for independence, France and Spain joined forces to make an attempt to seize Gibraltar from the British in what became known as the Great Siege. Britain was ultimately successful in its defense of Gibraltar.

It was during the Great Siege that British workers began excavating tunnels that would give them access to strategic positions along the perimeter of Gibraltar.

The tunnels were built entirely by hand with sledgehammers, chisels, crowbars and gunpowder for blasting. By the end of the Siege, the length of the network of tunnels had reached 370 feet. Over the years, the tunnels were continually expanded up to and including the time of World War II.

With the outbreak of World War II, British leaders fully expected a German attack on Gibraltar because of its strategic location. As in time before, the control of Gibraltar meant control of the entrance to and exit from the Mediterranean. To defend the position, British and Canadian engineers constructed a massive 32-mile long network of tunnels to add to the existing tunnels enabling them to construct a "fortress within a fortress, a city within a city".

### Operation Felix

The British concerns were confirmed as Nazi leaders developed "Operation Felix", a plan designed to capture Gibraltar in three days. Inasmuch as Gibraltar was practically impenetrable from the sea and had already shown to be able to withstand aerial assaults, Operation Felix was predicated on a land attack through Spain.

To accomplish this, Hitler had to deal with Spanish dictator Francisco Franco. While Spain remained officially neutral during the war, Hitler and Franco had provided aid to each other in earlier years.

# Gibraltar (16)

Operation Felix ultimately failed because Hitler and Franco had a mutual lack of trust for each other. Both men were belligerent in their dealings with each other and Felix never got off the ground.

### Operation Tracer

Operation Tracer was developed by British Naval Intelligence as a strategic counter-measure to the expected Nazi attack. Gibraltar was simply too important to leave it vulnerable to the Germans.

Operation Tracer was the brainchild of Rear Admiral John Henry Godfrey, the Director of the Naval Intelligence Division of the British Admiralty. In 1941, he decided to **establish a covert observation post at Gibraltar that would remain operational even if Gibraltar fell to the enemy.** with just one mission; to spy on German forces and radio London with their findings.

The men assigned to the post were assigned to a one-year mission, but were given provisions for seven years with the understanding that there would be no guarantees on the actual length of service.

*The plan was to entomb a group of men indefinitely inside the rock of Gibraltar*

Operation tracer called for six (6) team members consisting of an Officer (Leader), two physicians and three telegraphists. [92]

---

[92] Interesting Note: Ian Fleming, writer of the James Bond novels, served as personal assistant to Rear Admiral Godfrey during the development of Operation Tracer.

| Arsenal

## Stay Behind Caves

The "Stay Behind Caves" were never used and orders were given to seal the caves on 24 August 1943 where they remained a mystery until their discovery in 1997.

> "It wasn't just a cave it was a complete purpose-built tunnel system within the existing tunnel system...

> "The floor of the main hall had been covered in cork tiles to reduce any noise and to provide some insulation and it was of sufficient dimensions to permit the men to exercise. At one end of the room, in the walls, they found a 10,000-gallon water tank filled from a water catchment high in the Rock. There was a brass tap in the wall with an area where the water could drain away naturally.

> "Going on from the main room towards a set of steps, the toilet area was discovered and opposite was what used to be the radio room. By the side of this room were the rusting remains of a bicycle A leather strap, probably to cut down on noise, had been used to replace the standard drive chain. This was used as a generator to recharge the radio batteries (and to give the men some other form of exercise). When it was the prearranged time to send their signal, to avoid any interference with contact with the rock, the aerial was fed down through an asbestos pipe. Immediately after the broadcast the aerial was brought back into the complex."
>
> **Neill Rush**[93]

The cave facilities included east and west facing observation posts with a hidden observation platform on the eastern opening. A copper aerial was designed to be suspended from a platform and was concealed after use by retracting it into a pipe that ran down along the stairs leading back down to the living quarters.

---

[93] Rush, Neill. "Operation Tracer – Stay Behind Caves", aboutourrock.com. About Our Rock. 19 May 2012.

## Gibraltar (16)

The west-facing opening was much smaller, affording only enough room for one observer to look through at a time, and was concealed from the outside by means of a concrete wedge that was placed in the opening when not in use.

The floor of the main living area was covered with cork, most likely for the purpose of concealing any sounds of the men moving around in the facility.

### Operation Torch

Gibraltar served as the Allied base of operation for the invasion of North Africa under the code name of "Operation Torch".

The plan was for 65,000 men, under the command of then Lt. General Dwight Eisenhower, to invade French North African possessions at Casablanca, Oran and Algiers where they would conduct an offensive against German forces led by Field Marshal Erwin Rommel.

At the end of October 1942, British Lt. General Bernard Montgomery's Eighth Army attacked the Germans at El Alamein, precipitating a massive battle of attrition that Axis forces had no hope of winning.

Against Hitler's orders, Rommel's forces began retreating into Libya by November, 1942.

### Joint High Command

From a military standpoint, Operation Torch was successful. From a political perspective, the Operation revealed leadership issues that would need to be addressed for the longer term. One of the unintended benefits was that it brought the British and American senior leaders together in a way that led to the establishment of an effective joint high command.

Allied staff officers and senior military leaders began working together to develop common practices, and even a common language for military operations. Eisenhower in particular benefited from the experience of leading a combined force of

| Arsenal

British and American ground, sea and air forces, laying the groundwork for the 1944 D-day invasion at Normandy.

Beginning in September 1943, British and American senior ground and air commanders began the process of transferring from the Mediterranean to London, to begin planning for Operation Overlord. Besides Eisenhower, Bernard Montgomery, Omar Bradley, George S. Patton, and James H. Doolittle all transferred from the Mediterranean to the Overlord operation.

Whatever the difficulties that would emerge in the command relationships during the campaigns in northwestern Europe during 1944 and 1945, they were at least manageable. Operation Torch provided 18 months of seasoning and forging of relationships among Allied leadership that would prove beneficial in the later years of the war.

While Gibraltar and Operation Torch provided time to strengthen and season Allied leadership in North Africa and the Mediterranean, they had the opposite effect on Germany's military capacity.

During those months of fighting, not only were the Nazi forces in the Mediterranean weakened, but the Germans also suffered defeats at Stalingrad, Kursk, and in the Ukraine seriously undermining German fighting power.

### Preparation for Battle

Allied leaders had wanted a much earlier date for the D-day Invasion of France. However, the additional time proved profitable to Allied leadership and greatly improved its probability for success. Through Operation Torch, leaders were developed and identified, command relationships were forged and the probability for Allied victory at Normandy was greatly enhanced.

Gibraltar (16)

# The Church (16.1)

"There is no greater drama in human record than the sight of a few Christians, scorned or oppressed by a succession of emperors, bearing all trials with a fierce tenacity, multiplying quietly, building order while their enemies generated chaos, fighting the sword with the word, brutality with hope, and at last defeating the strongest state that history has known. Caesar and Christ had met in the arena, and Christ had won."

**Will Durant** [94]

In **Matthew 16:13-16** we find Jesus' conversation with the disciples where he asks them "Who do men say that I am?" and the follow up question "Who do you say that I am".

When Peter answers "You are the Christ, the Son of the living God", Jesus calls Peter "The Rock", and follows with the statement: "And on this Rock, I will build my church, and the gates of Hell will not prevail against it" (Matthew 16:18).

**What does this passage tell us about the power and importance of the "Church"?**

_____
_____
_____

**What are the implications of verse 19?**

_____
_____
_____

---

[94] Durant, Will, *The Story of Civilization Part III, Caesar and Christ*, New York, Simon & Schuster, 1944

| Arsenal

## "Bride of Christ" (16.2)

In Ephesians 5, the Apostle Paul instructs wives to be submissive to their husbands and husbands to love their wives as Christ loved the church and gave himself up for her. The passage concludes with:

> "This mystery is profound, and I am saying that it refers to Christ and the church." **Ephesians 5:32**

Read **Ephesians 5:22-33** and comment on the love of Christ for his bride. Note the specific details that demonstrate that love.

_____

_____

_____

> "Then I heard what seemed to be the voice of a great multitude, like the roar of many waters and like the sound of mighty peals of thunder, crying out,
>
> "Hallelujah!
> For the Lord our God the Almighty reigns.
> ⁷ Let us rejoice and exult and give him the glory,
> for the marriage of the Lamb has come,
> and his Bride has made herself ready;
> ⁸ it was granted her to clothe herself
> with fine linen, bright and pure"—
> for the fine linen is the righteous
> deeds of the saints.
>
> ⁹ And the angel said to me, "Write this: Blessed are those who are invited to the marriage supper of the Lamb."
> **Revelation 19:6-10**

The Church is the bride of Christ. He gave his life for her. He has promised to protect, preserve, and sanctify her.

Gibraltar (16)

## **Militant Church (16.3)**

"Essentially, the church is, was, and always will be a single worshiping community, permanently gathered in the true sanctuary which is the heavenly Jerusalem, the place of God's presence. Here all who are alive in Christ, the physically living with the physically dead (i.e., the church militant with the church triumphant) worship continually. In the world, however, this one church appears in the form of local congregations, each one called to fulfill the role of being a microcosm (a small-scale representative sample) of the church as a whole. This explains how it is that for Paul the one church universal is the body of Christ and so is the local congregation."

**James I Packer** [95]

Notice Packer's choice of the terms "church triumphant" and "church militant". What images come to mind when you see those words:

_____

_____

**Read Ephesians 4:11-16**
What is the call of the "visible church"?

_____

_____

_____

The church "triumphant" consists of Believers who have graduated to their eternal reward, and is made up of only true followers of Christ. The "militant church" consists of true Believers within the "visible church" who are still engaged in the Spiritual battle.

---

[95] Packer, J.I., *Concise Theology*, Foundation for Reformation, 1993, Orlando, Florida

| Arsenal

## The Call to Worship (16.4)

Someone tells you "Going to church doesn't get you to heaven", "We are saved by grace alone, so going to church isn't necessary to be a Christian", or the classic line "Sitting in church doesn't make you a Christian any more than sitting in a garage makes you a car".

**How do you respond?**

**Acts 2:42-47** _____

_____

_____

> "His intent was that now, through the church, the manifold wisdom of God should be made known to the rulers and authorities in the heavenly realms, according to his eternal purpose that he accomplished in Christ Jesus our Lord"
> **Ephesians 3:10-11**

Webster defines "manifold" as "comprehending or uniting various features". In light of this definition, how would you describe the role of the church as described in **Ephesians 3:10-11**?

_____

_____

_____

> "Let us hold fast the confession of our hope without wavering, for he who promised is faithful. And let us consider how to stir up one another to love and good works, not neglecting to meet together, as is the habit of some, but encouraging one another, and all the more as you see the Day drawing near."
> **Hebrews 10:23-25**

Gibraltar (16)

## **Equipping of the Saints (16.5)**

"And he gave the apostles, the prophets, the evangelists, the shepherds and teachers,[12] to equip the saints for the work of ministry, for building up the body of Christ, [13] until we all attain to the unity of the faith and of the knowledge of the Son of God, to mature manhood, to the measure of the stature of the fullness of Christ, [14] so that we may no longer be children, tossed to and fro by the waves and carried about by every wind of doctrine, by human cunning, by craftiness in deceitful schemes. [15] Rather, speaking the truth in love, we are to grow up in every way into him who is the head, into Christ, [16] from whom the whole body, joined and held together by every joint with which it is equipped, when each part is working properly, makes the body grow so that it builds itself up in love."-

**Ephesians 4:11-16**

From this passage, can you summarize the purpose and work of the Church? _____
_____
_____
_____

"Unto this catholic and visible Church, Christ hath given the ministry, oracles, and ordinances of God, **for the gathering and perfecting of the saints,** in this life, to the end of the world; and doth by his own presence and Spirit, according to his promise, make them effectual thereunto."

**Westminster Confession of Faith** [96]

---

[96] Sproul, R C. Truths We Confess, a Layman's Guide to the Westminster Confession of Faith. Phillipsburg, NJ: P&R Publishing, 2006.

| Arsenal

## **Presenting His Bride (16.6)**

"Husbands, love your wives, as Christ loved the church and gave himself up for her, 26 that he might sanctify her, having cleansed her by the washing of water with the word, 27 so that he might present the church to himself in splendor, without spot or wrinkle or any such thing, that she might be holy and without blemish."

**Ephesians 5:25-27**

What is the promise of Christ to his church?

_____

_____

How is this promise carried out in these passages?

**Matthew 18:15-21**  _____

**1 Corinthians 5**  _____

_____

_____

Sanctification necessarily includes discipline. We use it to protect and prepare our children for life. It is an act of grace and love when the church addresses sin in the life of a Believer. Its purpose is two-fold:

One purpose is to protect the purity and peace of the church. In 1 Corinthians 5, Paul expresses displeasure that the church has not dealt with a man caught in grievous sin, in part because of its infectious potential ("a little leaven leavens the whole lump").

The second purpose addresses our role in the growth and sanctification of others, a process that includes teaching, encouragement, mentoring, reproof, correction and – yes, discipline.

Gibraltar (16)

# "Visible" and "Invisible" (16.7)

"This catholic (*universal*) Church hath been sometimes more, sometimes less, visible. And particular Churches, which are members thereof, are more or less pure, according as the doctrine of the gospel is taught and embraced, ordinances administered, and public worship performed more or less purely in them."
**Westminster Confession of Faith** [97]

Read **Matthew 7:15-27**
What are the warnings and how should we respond?

_____

_____

_____

The term "invisible" does not mean we don't display the fruits that should be evident in the life of every true Believer. We use the term "invisible church" to refer to the body of all **true** Believers living on earth or in Heaven.

The "visible church" is the group of people who identify themselves as "Christians". That group includes both true followers of Christ and those who have not yet made a true profession of faith in Christ as Lord and Savior.

> "When the Son of Man comes in his glory, and all the angels with him, then he will sit on his glorious throne. [32] Before him will be gathered all the nations, and he will separate people one from another as a shepherd separates the sheep from the goats."
> **Matthew 25: 31-32**

---

[97] Sproul, R C. *Truths We Confess, a Layman's Guide to the Westminster Confession of Faith*. Phillipsburg, NJ: P&R Publishing, 2006.

| Arsenal

## **Special Orders (16.8)**

While it is true that "we do not get to heaven on the basis of our church membership", Scripture makes it abundantly clear that Christ has chosen to use his Church as his primary means to preserve, protect, equip, and sanctify his elect.

> "Let us hold fast the confession of our hope without wavering, for he who promised is faithful. And let us consider how to stir up one another to love and good works, not neglecting to meet together, as is the habit of some, but encouraging one another, and all the more as you see the Day drawing near."
> **Hebrews 10:23-25**

Christ has called us to be involved in a congregation of Believers who meet together regularly to worship, "stir up" and encourage one another.

### **Worship**

We are called to worship Christ in everything we do, both in and out of the Church. But Christ has ordained His Church to be the primary means for gathering His people for corporate worship.

Jesus should be the focal point of all worship and he has chosen his Bride as the primary means of bringing Christians together for that purpose. He has called us not to neglect the regular assembly.

### **Equipping**

Christ has ordained His Church to stand firm against the "Gates of Hell". It is the central staging point for all spiritual warfare. In and through the Church, we are trained for the battle and deployed to do Christ's work. In and through the Church we are called to be equipped through fellowship, discipline, accountability, training and education.

Through the Church, Christ has equipped pastors, teachers, and shepherds to guide His flock. He has structured His Church to be an incubator for relational accountability, encouragement and edification of others, service to each other, and a model for true Christian love.

He has called his Church to be the central staging ground for evangelism and outreach. From the Church, members are deployed as missionaries to spread the gospel locally and around the world. The Church is the place where Christians are equipped for various ministries of service and it is to the Church that we turn to for encouragement and rest from the battles against the world, the flesh and the devil.

## Imperfect Bride

The "Bride of Christ" is the true Church. He established it with his sacrifice on the Cross. He has promised to preserve and protect her for all eternity. He has promised to sanctify her and present her faultless in all her radiant beauty.

As members of the visible church, we face criticism when our walk falls short of what we profess. Indeed, that is part of the spiritual battle. This fact further emphasizes the need for the body of Christ to stand with us in that battle.

In Matthew 13, Jesus uses the "Parable of the Soils", the "Parable of the Weeds", and the "Parable of the Net" to remind us that, in its present state, the "visible" Church includes a number of members who identify themselves as Christians but have never truly surrendered to Christ.

We are faced with both a challenge and an opportunity with those in our midst who are not true Believers. Some of the "weeds" have been planted by Satan and their goal is to disrupt and damage the work and witness of the Church. Ultimately, it is Christ alone who will deal with the "weeds" who have grown up among us.

Other non-believers in our midst may be there for social reasons and others seeking solutions to issues in their own lives. The challenge comes from an outward profession that is devoid of the power of the indwelling Holy Spirit. The opportunity comes when the Church becomes the vessel by which many of them will come to true repentance and faith.

## Arsenal

A second challenge comes from those of us who are true Believers and continue do and say things that bring dishonor to the cause of Christ and draw the attention of a watching world eager to see us fall.

In its present state, the "visible church" is not the perfect bride. But Christ has chosen her and He will cleanse her and present her faultless.

According to the Westminster Confession of Faith:

> "The purest Churches under heaven are subject both to mixture and error: and some have so degenerated as to become apparently no Churches of Christ. **Nevertheless, there shall be always a Church on earth, to worship God according to his will**"

### Spiritual Battlefield

Old Testament religious leaders were expecting a Messiah who would come in as a victorious leader who would deliver them from Roman captivity. Instead, Jesus came in to prepare followers to defeat a much stronger enemy – the world, the flesh and the devil.

He selected leaders to build his Church. He taught them, trained them, and equipped them for a mission with eternal consequences. He promised to build a church, his people, for whom he and he alone would become the Cornerstone and against whom the "gates of Hell" would never prevail.

As we seek to do his work on the Spiritual battlefield, we rely on various "disciplines of grace" as our weapons of warfare. The Church is our central "staging" ground for those weapons.

**Without the Church,
our shields are porous, the sword is dull,
and the breastplate is nothing more than a
cosmetic covering.**

# U.S.S. Hornet (17)

Imagine being the first pilot tasked with taking off or landing from an aircraft carrier. No catapult to assist you in takeoff and upon landing, nothing to keep you from running off the end of the ship.

Given the simple design of the airplane at the time the first carrier was built in 1920, it would have been difficult to envision the impact that the aircraft carrier would have on military operations during and following World War II.

The USS Jupiter was commissioned on 7 April 1913, as a bulk cargo ship designed to transport coal to keep other ships in fuel. She was "state-of-the-art", in her design, and an experiment to improve safety to reduce the risk of fire from the coal dust she carried.

But the USS Jupiter is most remembered for her role in history by her transformation in 1920 as the nation's first aircraft carrier – commissioned on 20 March 1920.

The transformation took the seven 50-foot tall towers of the Jupiter and used them to support the flight deck. There was no control tower. Take-off and landing would be largely left to the skills of the pilot.

The ship's first executive officer, Kenneth Whiting, had been personally trained as a pilot by Orville Wright.

The first flight from the deck of the Langley took place on 17 October 1922. The ship's first landing came nine days later.

| Arsenal

The Langley was sunk by the Japanese in February, 1942 but its successors played a pivotal role in the Pacific theater, allowing American fighter planes and bombers to get close enough to do the work needed for the eventual defeat of the Empire of Japan.

USS Jupiter - 1913

Transformation – from cargo ship to aircraft carrier

USS Langley - 1920

## U.S.S. Hornet

**Admiral Yamamoto**

In the months following Pearl Harbor, the Japanese scored major victories throughout the Pacific, including Malaysia, the Dutch East Indies, the Philippines, and Singapore. Fleet Admiral Isoruku Yamamoto enjoyed naval superiority at the time but feared that, given enough time and resources, U.S. naval forces would grow to exceed his own.

# U.S.S. Hornet (17)

Admiral Yamamoto's strategy was centered around an early destruction of the U.S. naval fleet, starting with the sinking of U.S. aircraft carriers and the seizing of Midway Island, the only strategic island other than Hawaii in the eastern Pacific. His carrier strike force had been reduced as a result of the Battle of Coral Sea in May, 1942. His success at Midway would be predicated on the element of surprise.

If successful, Yamamoto's plan would destroy the U.S. Pacific Fleet and provide a forward outpost from which the Japanese could eliminate any future American threat in the Central Pacific.

Yamamoto's plan for Midway included a diversionary operation on the Aleutian Islands west of Alaska. But that diversion further divided his resources. That operation was temporarily successful as Japan captured the islands of Attu and Kiska.

Strategically, it did not produce the intended results of diverting American naval resources away from Midway. America had broken a key Japanese naval code and was aware of Yamamoto's plans.

## Japanese Fleet

The Japanese fleet included four (4) of the aircraft carriers that had performed so well at Pearl Harbor: the **Akagi**, the **Hiryu**, the **Kaga**, and the **Soryu**, accompanied by two (2) battleships: the Haruna and the Kirishima. They proceeded as an integrated battle group with their speed constrained by the top speed of the battleships.

The US fleet included the carriers: **USS Hornet**, the **USS Enterprise**, and the **USS Yorktown**.

Japanese aerial forces were estimated at 108 planes, consisting of 36 each, level bombers, dive bombers and fighter planes.

| Arsenal

On the American side, Midway was defended by the Marine Fighting Squadron 221 (VMF-221), with 20 flying "Brewster Buffalos" and seven (7) Grumman Wildcats. Marine squadron (VMF-241) were equipped with 11 Vought Vindicators and 16 Douglass Dauntlesses.

**Brewster Buffalo**

The U.S. Army Air Force (7th Army Air Force Detachment) was equipped with four (4) B-26 Martin Marauders and 19 B-17 Flying Fortresses.

**Midway**
4 June 1942 – 0430 hours:
The Japanese launched their initial air attack against Midway using dive-bombers, torpedo bombers, and fighters. At the same time, they launched several reconnaissance aircraft to search for any possible U.S. Navy ships in the area. Poor weather kept them from locating the nearby American fleet.

In the early stages of the battle, USMC planes were no match for the much faster Japanese Zeros, and most were shot down shortly after takeoff. By 6:20 am, the U.S. base at Midway had been bombed and was heavily damaged. While fighter planes were engaging the Zeros, USAAF bombers had already been deployed to attack the Japanese carrier fleet.

Early Japanese success proved to be short-lived, as the attack did not succeed in neutralizing Midway. American bombers could still use the air base to attack the Japanese ground invasion force. While the Japanese planned another attack for 7 June 1942, the aerial attacks on Midway Island left its carriers vulnerable to American bomber attacks at sea.

**At Sea**
4 June 1942 – 0700 Hours
Having taken off prior to the Japanese attack, American bombers based on Midway attacked the Japanese carrier fleet. These

## U.S.S. Hornet (17)

included six brand new Grumman TBF Avengers from Hornet's VT-8 torpedo squadron that had been transiting Midway. The Japanese air defense were able to destroy all but one of Hornet's TBFs and two Army bombers.

U.S. carriers were ordered to begin launching their aircraft to strike the Japanese fleet, while Japanese carrier crews were busy re-arming their aircraft with general purpose bombs for use against the remaining targets on Midway. This decision left them ill-suited to defend their own carriers.

### 0920 Hours

TBD Devastator torpedo bombers launched from the USS Hornet attacked the Japanese fleet. Every plane was shot down without scoring any hits on the Japanese. The only American airman to survive the attacks was Ensign George Gay.

Shortly thereafter, another group of TBD Devastator bombers were launched from the USS Enterprise, with similar results. By the time torpedo bombers had been launched from the USS Yorktown, three (3) squadrons of "Dauntless" bombers were overhead.

U.S. torpedo squadrons suffered enormous losses in the attack on the Japanese fleet. However, their sacrifices were not in vain as they took the Japanese forces down to sea level, delayed rearmament of aircraft intended for Midway, and set the table for American dive bombers to strike the Japanese carriers with impunity.

Armed aircraft filled the Japanese hangar decks, fuel hoses snaked across the decks as refueling operations were underway, and bombs and torpedoes were stacked around the hangars, rather than stowed safely in the magazines. All of this made the Japanese carriers extraordinarily vulnerable.

Within minutes, three of the four Japanese carriers (**Kaga**, **Akagi**, and **Soryu**) had been severely damaged by bombs and were out of action. Within hours, they were abandoned and sank. The surviving carrier, **Hiryu**, launched a counter-strike that badly

| Arsenal

damaged the **USS Yorktown**. Later in the afternoon, dive bombers from **USS Enterprise** hit the carrier **Hiryu** and left her fatally ablaze.

7 June 1942, **Yorktown** was torpedoed by a Japanese submarine and sank. The battle was over and Midway was still in American hands.

**The Aftermath**
The Battle of Midway permanently damaged the Japanese carrier fleet and the loss of operational capability during this critical phase of the campaign ultimately proved decisive. The Japanese were incapable of replacing the lost carriers.

Because of the irreparable damage to the Japanese carrier force, the U.S. moved up its efforts to liberate nations that had been conquered by Japan. Just two months after Midway, U.S. Marines landed on Guadalcanal in the Solomon Islands.

America's victory at Midway, and successive victories in the Pacific theatre were the result of American superiority in the air. But air superiority would not have been possible without the aircraft carriers that served as bases for their operations.

The USS Hornet had already served as a base of operation for Colonel Doolittle, who relied on the carrier to take his 16 Mitchell B-25s into Tokyo in April, 1942. At Midway, the Hornet was joined by the Enterprise and Yorktown and served as the bases for the American aerial victory there. Of the three carriers, only the USS Enterprise would survive the war. But all of them had served their purpose.

The aircraft carrier was critical to the war in the Pacific. They transported our aircraft and pilots to the battle. Without them, our aircraft did not have the range to reach their targets.

Following each engagement, the carrier provided a place for pilots to rest, rehabilitate, rearm, refuel, redeploy... and ultimately to return home from their missions.

U.S.S. Hornet (17)

## Amazing Grace (17.1)

There seems to be a growing belief that the Christian life is like a vacation on a cruise ship. The well-worn phrase "Let go and Let God" is not in the Bible. Scripture calls us to "strive", to "press on", to "stand firm" – and that doesn't sound much like sitting around waiting for "grace" to happen. We are being equipped for a battle, not a vacation on the beach.

On the other hand, as Believers seeking to develop the disciplines of grace, we can easily fall into a "bootstraps" mentality that will eventually lead to failure and frustration. Our power source is not in our own strength, stamina and intelligence.

On the spiritual battlefield, we are called to "fight the good fight of faith" but we do so only with the enabling power of God's grace; without which we are like the bomber over the Pacific – completely exposed to the enemy and unequipped for the mission. Scripture calls us to actively "pursue" holiness (100% effort) relying (100%) on God's grace as the power that drives that transformation.

In **Pilgrim's Progress**, Christian encounters two men on the road by the name of Formalist and Hypocrisy. They came from the land of Vainglory and they were headed for the Celestial City. The two men were approaching the gates of the city by another route. Christian's message to them was:

> "By laws and ordinances you will not be saved, since you came in not by the door. As for this coat that is on my back, it was given to me by the Lord of the place wither I go, and that, as you say, to cover my nakedness with" [98]

Like Christian, as we approach the Celestial City, we are clothed only with grace.

---

[98] Bunyan, John, *Pilgrims Progress*, Vintage Publishers, New York, NY, 2004

| Arsenal

## Sola Gratia (17.1)

As Believers, we should already be aware that salvation comes by grace alone, through faith alone, in Christ alone. All of our works are like "filthy rags" (**Isaiah 64:6**) and play no role in our salvation and adoption as children of God.

As we pursue righteousness; as we seek to become closer in our walk with Christ, we cannot forget the source of our salvation is the gospel of grace.

What is the relationship between our salvation and our "works" (church attendance, ministry activities, the tithe, Bible studies, etc.)?

**Ephesians 2:4-10** _____
**2 Timothy 1:8-10** _____
_____
_____

**Acts 15:5-12** _____
_____

**Romans 3:19-26** _____
_____

In the passages above take note of our condition before God called us by His grace:

In Ephesians 2:5, Paul does not say we were "sin-sick". We were dead in our sins. We were totally incapable of lifting a finger to assist in our own salvation. 2 Timothy 1:9 tells us that His grace was initiated "before the ages began".

In Acts 15 and Romans 3 we are called to avoid the temptation to add our works, in any form, to receive God's justification. Grace is an act of God alone, initiated by him alone, and we dare not rely on any act of our own as the basis for our salvation... not circumcision, not baptism, confirmation, nor communion. Bible memory, keeping of the tithe, teaching, preaching, speaking in tongues or any deeds of mercy that we may be involved in play no role in our justification.

> "What then shall we say was gained by Abraham, our forefather according to the flesh? For if Abraham was justified by works, he has something to boast about, but not before God. For what does the Scripture say? "Abraham believed God, and it was counted to him as righteousness." Now to the one who works, his wages are not counted as a gift but as his due. And to the one who does not work but believes in him who justifies the ungodly, his faith is counted as righteousness"
>
> **Romans 4 1-5**

Note the use of the term "wages", that are paid to us in return for our labor. Wages are earned, and wages cease when we stop working. Contrast the term wages from "gifts" which are freely given by the giver without condition.

True Believers are chosen by God before the foundation of the world and are called to receive salvation by grace alone through faith alone in Christ alone.

> "We are saved by faith alone,
> but the faith that saves
> is never alone"
> **Martin Luther**

| Arsenal

## **Vigorous Pursuit of Holiness (17.2)**

"The pursuit of holiness requires sustained and vigorous effort. It allows for no indolence, no lethargy, no half-hearted commitment, and no laissez faire attitude toward even the smallest sins. In short, it demands the highest priority in the life of a Christian, because to be holy is to be like Christ – God's goal for every Christian"

**Jerry Bridges** [99]

What do the following passages tell us about the grace/works relationship?

**Romans 5:20 - 6:4**
**Romans 6:12-16**

_____
_____
_____
_____
_____
_____
_____

"Being a Christian doesn't mean you and I don't sin anymore. We will still sin, but sin ceases to be the predominant pattern of our lives. That's because as Christians, we are new creatures in Christ"

**Jim George** [100]

---

[99] Bridges, Jerry, *The Discipline of Grace*, 1994, NaviPress Publishing, Colorado Springs, Co

[100] George, Jim, *A Man After God's Own Heart*, Harvest House Publishers 2002, Eugene, Oregon

U.S.S. Hornet (17)

## **The Power of Grace (17.3)**

If we acknowledge the fact that our salvation was entirely the result of God's grace, how does grace serve to equip us on the spiritual battlefield?

**Galatians 2:19-21**
**John 15:4-5**
**Titus 2:11-14**

> "We are his workmanship, created in Christ Jesus for good works with God prepared beforehand that we would walk in them"
>
> **Ephesians 2:10**

Notice how we are dependent on God's grace for everything we do. Before we became Christians, our lives were driven by the power of the world, the flesh, and the devil. Once we became followers of Jesus Christ, the power source in our life changed. Our lives are being transformed by the enabling power of God's grace.

> "Grace is the pleasure of God to magnify the worth of God by giving sinners the right and power to delight in God without obscuring the glory of God."
> **John Piper** [101]

---

[101] Piper, John, *The Pleasures of God: Meditations on God's Delight in Being God*, Doubleday Religious Publication Group, 2012

| Arsenal

## **Performance Mentality (17.4)**

> Your worst days are never so bad that you are beyond the reach of God's grace, and your best days are never so good that you are beyond the need of God's grace" –
>
> **Jerry Bridges** [102]

You can't believe you are having a terrible day at work – after such a great quiet time this morning. You took out the garbage without being reminded, you prayed with a friend over the phone and you gave 2 bucks to the guy at the end of the exit ramp.

Yesterday, you woke up too late for your quiet time, yelled at your wife on the way out the door and caused the "idiot" on the highway to wonder why you have a fish on your bumper. Now a friend is calling for encouragement and you feel so unworthy to offer up a prayer on his behalf.

Writing to Titus, Paul instructs us on the manner of life we should live as image bearers of Christ:

**Titus 2:1-10** _____

_____

What is the power that instructs and trains us for that life?

**Titus 2:11-14** _____

_____

It is easy to fall into the trap of expecting a "good or bad day" based on our Spiritual performance. But God does not love us any more on a "good day" than on a bad one. We live out the Spiritual battle on a moment by moment basis, relying on God's grace every step of the way.

---

[102] Bridges, Jerry, "*The Discipline of Grace*", NaviPress Publishing, 1994, Colorado Springs

U.S.S. Hornet (17)

# Special Orders (17.5)

Many of us run from one extreme to the other. We acknowledge salvation by "grace" alone but we live each day in the power of our own flesh to grow and mature in the Christian faith. At the other end of the spectrum are those of us who turn everything over to Christ and "wait" for him to do the work of spiritual growth and maturity without making any effort on our own.

Scripture tells us that we are totally dependent on Christ – not only for our salvation, but our maturity and growth. It is by grace that God enables us to grow. Yet the Bible also tells us to "run the race", "strive", "endure", "pursue holiness", "resist" the devil, "flee" temptation, etc. Those are action words.

There is a natural tension in the "grace-works" relationship that is difficult to reconcile.

**Consider the Farmer**

The fruit of his produce resides in its seed. God controls what can come from that seed. The farmer has nothing to say in the matter. God alone causes the seed to become a fruit producing plant. God, alone created the ingredients that make a strawberry different from an ear of corn.

Yet God has ordered the farmer's lifestyle to be very active in the process. He prepares the soil, plants the seeds, battles the insects, weeds, and disease. He is called to water and fertilize the plants and harvest the fruit.

While he is waiting for the harvest, the farmer is not sitting on the front porch. His "Waiting" is a time for repairing equipment, mending fences, or preparing another field. "Waiting on the Lord", is not a call to "let go and let God". It is a call to vigorously pursue righteousness without losing sight of the fact that we are HIS workmanship and He alone will bring for the harvest.

| Arsenal

**Spiritual Battlefield**
Satan is always close at hand when we move toward either extreme. When your spiritual "performance" is down for the day, the enemy is there with a voice of condemnation:
- "You are not worthy!"
- "How can you call yourself a Christian!"
- "You are not good enough to teach",
- "God is not listening to your prayers!"

At the opposite extreme, when we seem to have it together spiritually (quiet times, regular church attendance, ministry activities, prayer life, etc.), Satan is telling you that God owes you and if God does not respond appropriately, Satan tells you that God does not care about your needs.

> "We are saved by faith alone, but the faith that saves in never alone"
> **Martin Luther**

From the moment of our salvation, God uses the same grace that saved us to work in and through us to sanctify and bring us closer to Christ. We are totally dependent on Christ, but He has not called us to sit on the sofa waiting for him to do the work. By grace, he has given us the Spiritual armor to fight, strive, and pursue the image of Christ.

He orders our Spiritual maturity and sanctification according to his own plan and provides each and every Spiritual discipline to accomplish his purpose.

Christ did not save us by grace and walk away. His grace was the power that defeated Satan, and by the same grace, we walk victorious on the spiritual battlefield.

## P51 Mustang (18)

"I'll never worry about meeting a FW 190 in a 51 since I was able to outturn, out dive and generally out-maneuver him at all altitudes, from 23,000 feet to the deck; I could follow him in anything and do a lot more besides."

**Richard D Bishop**,
1st Lt, Air Corps–
11 September 1944 Saalfield, Germany.

**1,500 Hp**
**437 MPH**

## The power to out run, out dive & out maneuver the best the enemy has to offer

"At the beginning of the battle I was obliged to leave my element leader, Lt Wolf, in order to break into three ME109's on my tail. Later I met Lt Wolf at about 10,000 ft. heading for the deck after two ME 109s. He, Lt Wolf, closed in on one, the ME 109 to the right and started in a turn to the left at about 1,000 feet. I was fairly far behind but I saw his bullets chew off about two feet of the 109's left wing. The ME 109 went into a flat spin and crashed. The pilot did not get out of the aircraft"

**Daniel Myers, 2nd Lt, Air Corps**.

| Arsenal

## Mustang

The North American Aviation P51 "Mustang" was arguably one of the most recognizable and celebrated aircraft used in World War II. It earned its reputation primarily in Europe where it had an inauspicious beginning and was under-utilized during the earlier years of the war, but proved itself time and again as the war continued on.

Today, the Mustang is one of the most popular "classic warbirds" still being restored, collected, and flown across the United States. It bears unique qualities in terms of design and maneuverability. When you take into account the smooth distinctive sound of the Rolls Royce Merlin engine, the P51 is clearly at the head of its class.

## European Theatre

In the European theatre, where Germany occupied most of the continent, Britain was the only place from which to stage any significant military attack on Germany. To make matters worse, in the early days of the war, Germany held clear superiority in terms of air power. Any eventual invasion of the European mainland would have to contend with the German Luftwaffe and its superior aircraft.

Originally, Allied leaders did not see any offensive potential for the P51 and similar aircraft. In fact, the P51 saw very little action until early 1943, when it was primarily used as an escort to drive the enemy away from allied bombers. Up until that time, Allied B-17s were experiencing significant losses from Luftwaffe fighters that were faster and more maneuverable.

Unlike its predecessors, the P51 Mustang had the range to escort the heavy bombers deep into German territory and back, and was superior to the Luftwaffe's own fighters in terms of speed and maneuverability.

In time, the P51 was found to be more than just an escort. It became an effective offensive weapon due to its ability to out run, out dive, and out maneuver the best fighters Germany could bring. The P51 proved its capacity to break the back of the

## P51 Mustang (18)

German Luftwaffe. The P51's success led to a decision to utilize the planes to engage and attack the enemy.

> "The P-51 Mustang was a truly significant aircraft, probably the best all-around fighter developed during World War II. It had a major impact in the European air war by helping to clear the skies of the Luftwaffe, permitting the invasion of the mainland and the defeat of Germany."
> **C.E. "Bud" Anderson** [103]

### Pacific Theatre

The P51 is more famous for its effectiveness in Europe, primarily because there were a number of more suitable alternatives for carrier based aircraft. However, the Mustang was instrumental in a number of battles in the Pacific, as well.

From bases in Okinawa and Iwo Jima, the Mustang was able to conduct ground attack sweeps against Japanese airfields and supply routes. The P51 also proved effective supporting British ground troops in Burma and, in 1945, it was used to attack occupied areas of China.

### Power plant

The P51 was equipped with a 1,500 hp Rolls-Royce Merlin fighter engine and is regarded as the one of the most important weapons in the European theatre. Its high altitude speed was 437 miles per hour and it was equipped with six 5" machine guns.

The introduction of "drop tanks" increased fuel capacity and range that enabled the Mustang to go deep into enemy territory and back. Prior to the P51, escort planes had a much shorter range and often left Allied bombers vulnerable to enemy attacks.

The first jet-powered aircraft to enter operational service was the German Messerschmitt ME-262, introduced late in the war. It came with great speed and range, but its vulnerability was in its

---

[103] Excerpts taken from an article from "Dispatch, the Commemorative Air Force Magazine" Fall 2004, C. E. Bud Anderson

| Arsenal

lack of maneuverability at low speeds during takeoff and landing – and that is where allied fighters in the P51 attacked.

**Origins**

In 1940 (prior to America's entry into the War) the British approached North American Aviation to license and build Curtiss P40 fighters for the Royal Air Force. North American responded by offering to design a better fighter. Production of the aircraft, named Mustang I by the British began the following year.

The P51 was originally designed as an "escort" to keep German aircraft away from allied bombers, and for tactical reconnaissance. As a fighter, the Mustang was limited to ground operations, as the original Allison engine had limited performance at higher altitudes. Over time, modifications were made to the P51 that enabled increased speed, agility, payload and range that made it one of the most potent allied weapons of World War II.

Eventually becoming one of the most effective weapons in World War II, the Mustang was a testimony to aviation engineering and creative ingenuity. Originally deployed as the P51A, the final version created was the P51H (the highest produced Mustang was the P51D).

The canopy was modified to improve pilot visibility. Originally armed with four (4) .50 caliber guns, the newer versions carried six (6) guns with 1,880 rounds of ammunition. A dorsal fin was added and the camber of the wings was modified to improve mobility. Finally, the Allison engine was replaced by the Rolls-Royce Merlin Engine that made the P51 the most effective fighter aircraft, at altitude, in the war.

> "To say P-51 Mustangs were successful would be an understatement. It is considered to be the best piston aircraft of World War II and became one of the world's aviation elite. A total of 14,819 Mustangs of all types were built for the USAAF. American Mustangs destroyed 4,950 enemy aircraft making them the highest scoring US fighter in the Europe Theater of Operations. They were used as dive-bombers, bomber escorts, ground-attackers, interceptors,

## P51 Mustang (18)

for photo-recon missions, trainers, transports (with a jump-seat), and after the war, high performance racers." [104]

The P51 Mustang had an astonishing success rate:
- Ratio for kills to losses: 19 kills for every 1 Mustang lost.
- The P51 Mustang is credited with the destruction of 4,950 German planes, more than any other Allied fighter. Some of these kills included the jet powered Messerschmitt 262.

"The P-51 was something else. It was an awful antagonist, in the truest sense of that word and we hated it. It could do everything we could do and do it much better" –
**German Ace - Walter Wolfrum**

---

[104] Dwyer, Larry – The Aviation History Online Museum, November 29, 2001

| Arsenal

## Teach us to Pray (18.1)

The P51 was originally conceived as an escort for bombers delivering their weapons in enemy territory. What the Allies discovered in the Mustang was a powerful weapon in and of itself.

### The power to outrun, out dive and out maneuver the best the enemy has to offer

Many Christians view prayer as a ritualistic discipline, reciting written or memorized phrases learned over the years. Others view prayer as an opportunity to bring God a list of their wants, needs and desires. If those are your views, you are missing out on an awesome opportunity to have an audience with the King of Kings.

"A man is powerful on his knees."
**Corrie ten Boom**

"Prayer is a sincere, sensible, affectionate pouring out of the heart or soul to God, through Christ, in the strength and assistance of the Holy Spirit, for such things as God has promised, or according to His Word, for the good of the church, with submission in faith to the will of God."
**John Bunyan**

"Sometimes when we do not receive comfort in our prayers, when we are broken and cast down, that is when we are really wrestling and prevailing in prayer."
**Charles H. Spurgeon**

"Prayer lays hold of God's plan and becomes the link between his will and its accomplishment on earth."
**Elisabeth Elliot**

## P51 Mustang (18)

"Work, work, from morning until late at night. In fact, I have so much to do that I shall have to spend the first three hours in prayer!"
**Martin Luther**

"Now in the morning, having risen a long while before daylight, He (Jesus) went out and departed to a solitary place; and there He prayed."
**Mark 1:35**

"The effectual fervent prayer of a righteous man availeth much"
**James 5:16** KJV

"Every circumstance of our life should call forth prayer of some kind so that we involve God in every aspect of our lives because we are a people who have nothing and who without Him can do nothing."
**Franklin Graham**

Our prayers are weapons critical to the daily battle with the world, the flesh and the devil. Jesus regularly retreated to a place of prayer. Moses, Abraham, Ezekiel, Daniel, Isaiah and other heroes of the faith would not consider engaging enemy without first going to God in prayer.

> Entering the Spiritual battlefield
> without prayer is like a soldier
> going into battle without his boots,
> helmet, or weapon.

| Arsenal

## Hallowed be Thy Name (18.2)

"Pray then like this: Our Father, which art in heaven, Hallowed be thy name"
**Matthew 6:9**

"Worship is to feel in your heart and express in some appropriate manner a humbling but delightful sense of admiring awe and astonished wonder and overpowering love in the presence of that most ancient Mystery, that Majesty which philosophers call the First Clause, but which we call Our Father Which Art in Heaven"
**A.W. Tozer** [105]

**Revelation 5:6-14** – Describe the scene in your own words.

_____
_____
_____
_____

"In the Bible, we have the full and adequate revelation of the vast scope of the divine nature...God's sovereignty, truth, holiness, wisdom, love, faithfulness, patience, mercy – illumined and made relevant to us by the Holy Spirit, will feed the flame of our worship"
***Oswald Sanders*** [106]

When we begin our prayers with an attitude of worship, we experience the awesome reverence of who God is. He is much more than a cosmic Santa Claus or a friend who is there for a casual conversation.

---

[105] Fant, D.J., *A.W. Tozer, Christian Publications*, Harrisburg, Pa 1964

[106] Sanders, Oswald, *Enjoying Intimacy with God*, Moody Press, Chicago, IL 1980

## P51 Mustang (18)

"Worship is not accomplished only by a transaction uttered in a prayer or wish. Worship is a posture of life that takes as its primary purpose the understanding of what it really means to love and revere God."
**Ravi Zacharias** [107]

Describe the scene in **Isaiah 6:1-8.**
What was Isaiah's response?

_____
_____
_____
_____
_____

"The glory of God shines most brightly, most fully, most beautifully in the manifestation of the glory of his grace. ...God decreed from all eternity to display the greatness of the glory of his grace for the enjoyment of his creatures, and he revealed to us that this is the ultimate aim and explanation of why there is sin and why there is suffering, and why there is a great and suffering Savior, Jesus Christ."
**John Piper** [108]

**Psalm 150**
Where, how and how often should we offer our praises to God?

_____
_____
_____
_____
_____

---

[107] Zacharias, Ravi, *Jesus Among Other Gods*, Thomas Nelson, Inc., 2000

[108] Piper, John and Taylor, Justin – *Suffering and the Sovereignty of God*, Crossway Books, Wheaton, Illinois 2006

| Arsenal

Worship initiates our entry into the Holy of Holies granted to us by Christ's shed blood on the Cross. Jesus taught his disciples to pray by beginning with worship: "Hallowed be thy name".

**Exodus 15:1-7**

Old Testament priests were not allowed to enter the Holy of Holies except for certain times and under very strict conditions. Because Christ ripped the veil that separated us from God, we now have access to the Father in and through our prayers.

That access should not be lightly regarded. We are still entering the most Holy place. It is not a casual conversation with a golf-buddy or an opportunity for negotiation for things we want. Prayer rightly begins with worship for who God is. He is worthy of all praise.

Self-centered prayer is nothing short of idolatry. God-centered prayer puts us prostrate on the floor at the feet of an almighty God who already knows our needs, and loves us enough to welcome us into his presence.

P51 Mustang (18)

## Forgive us our debts (18.3)

The importance of confession "is not the meticulous observance of external ritual but the state of the offeror's heart. That is the sacrifice in which God finds delight, and that renders continuing intimacy with him possible."

**J. Oswald Sanders** [109]

**Satan's Device**

"to keep souls in a sad, doubting, and questioning condition, and so making their life a hell...to mind their sins as to forget, yea to neglect their Saviour. Their eyes so fixed upon their disease that they cannot see the remedy; though it be near."

**Thomas Brooks** [110]

Read **1 John 1:7- 2:2** How does this passage address "Satan's device" (above)?

_____
_____
_____

Is there a contradiction between **I John 2:1 and I John 1:8**?

_____
_____

Confession is much more than the intellectual acknowledgement of our sin. True confession comes with a sincere, broken heart – even if it's a sin you just committed for the tenth time today. Brooks' challenge to us is to redirect our focus. Satan seeks to overwhelm us with our guilt. Christ is calling us to himself.

---

[109] Sanders, J. Oswald, *Enjoying Intimacy with God*, Moody Press, Chicago, IL 1980

[110] Brooks, Thomas, *Precious Remedies against Satan's Devices* (Carlisle, Pa : The Banner of Truth Trust, 1652

| Arsenal

"There is a common and dangerous tendency among us to 'cover' our sins. We may go to church and join in the general confession, and in our private prayers say we are sorry for our sins. But our words have a hollow sound...We know little of the uncomfortable discipline of confessing and forsaking our sins, so finding mercy." [111] -
**John Stott**

**Psalm 32:1-5** - Describe David's attitude in his confession

_____

_____
_____
_____
_____

"If we confess our sins, he is faithful and just to forgive us our sins and cleanse us from all unrighteousness"
**I John 1:9**

On the Spiritual battlefield, one of Satan's most effective weapons is unconfessed sin. When we cover, dismiss, minimize, rationalize or justify our sins, we give Satan the opportunity to hold us. Then he works to imprison us in despair and defeat.

David's own words from Psalm 32:3:

**"When I kept silent,
my bones wasted away"**

---

[111] Stott, John - *Confess Your Sins*, (Waco, Texas), Word, 1974 - quote taken *from Enjoying Intimacy with God*, by Oswald Sanders

P51 Mustang (18)

## **Standing Stones (18.4)**

We come into his presence with our petitions and our needs and he hears our prayers. The part of our prayer that starts with worship and confession then thanksgiving sets the tone of the rest of the prayer, an awesome reverence for God and a reminder of all He has done in our lives.

**1 Samuel 7:10-13** describes the "Ebenezer" stone:

> "Then Samuel took a stone and set it up between Mizpah and Shen and called its name Ebenezer; for he said, 'Till now the Lord has helped us.' So the Philistines were subdued and did not again enter the territory of Israel. And the hand of the Lord was against the Philistines all the days of Samuel."
> **1 Samuel 7:12-13**

**Joshua 4:1-7** _____

**Joshua 4:18-24** _____

_____

> "Joshua used stones to help God's people remember His goodness. After wandering in the wilderness for 40 years, the Israelites experienced the power of God to roll back the waters of the Jordan River, enabling them to cross over and take possession of the Promised Land. Joshua then commanded them to build a memorial of stones as a public testimony of what God had done for them ... stones that would remind them to keep on praising Him"
> **Anne Graham Lotz** [112]

When the people saw the stones stacked up by the Jordan, they had a tangible, physical reminder of God's faithfulness. While we may not use stones today, there are things we can do to remind us of the times when God showed up in a powerful way.

---

[112] Lotz, Anne Graham, "The Stones of Remembrance", January 29, 2009, Billy Graham Evangelistic Association

| Arsenal

Sometimes, the "Oh wow!", moments in our lives provide a basis for remembering the height and breadth of his provision. Those memories should evoke a grateful attitude that goes well beyond a simple "thank you".

**Exodus 12:40-51**
The annual celebration of the Passover was God's reminder to Israel of his deliverance from the captivity of Egypt.

_____
_____
_____

**Exodus 15:1-13**
Can you remember God's provision or deliverance from a very difficult challenge in life?

_____
_____

**Exodus 16:31-35**
Do you have an omer of manna around your house today?

_____
_____

Many of us will find ourselves in a "routine" of ritual prayers of thanksgiving. In and of themselves, there is certainly nothing unbiblical for thanking God for our families, our jobs, our homes and our provision of daily bread. But the tangible reminder, the "stone of remembrance" takes it to a whole new level.

P51 Mustang (18)

# Thy Will be done (18.5)

"Prayer is a sincere, sensible, affectionate pouring out of the heart or soul to God, through Christ, in the strength and assistance of the Holy Spirit, for such things as God has promised, or according to His Word, for the good of the church, with submission in faith to the will of God."

**John Bunyan**

There are some who claim that praying "if it be thy will" reveals a lack of faith... that faith as small as a mustard seed can move mountains. But only God knows if moving that mountain is a good idea. Faith in God's power should also be accompanied by faith in God's wisdom. "Thy will be done" is a powerful statement of faith.

Suppose you are building an airplane in your driveway and your next door neighbor, an expert airplane builder, comes over to help. He offers some suggestions to make the plane more airworthy.

Hopefully you would not ask him to keep is opinions to himself. You would listen to a man who understands aerodynamics and can tell you how to keep the plane in the air. You asked for and received **both his physical help and his wisdom and knowledge**.

Do you hesitate to ask "Thy Will Be Done" in your prayers? If so, what is your primary fear?

_____

_____

When we pray "Thy will be done", we are inviting God to be a part of every element of our prayer. If the answer is "no", we accept it because we trust His infinite wisdom and His unfailing love.

**Romans 8:26-28** - What is it that ties our desires to the will of God? _____

_____

_____

Warrior 257

# Arsenal

"The purpose of prayer is not to change God's mind but to change ours, to bring us into communion with him, to come to our heavenly Father andtell him what is on our hearts. He invites us-no he commands and encourages us to do that"

**R.C. Sproul** [113]

**Matthew 7:7**
"Ask and ye shall receive" is a verse that many like to quote. Read verse 11 and put this promise in context.

_____

_____

_____

What does **James 4:1-10** say about unanswered prayers?

_____

_____

"The spiritual quality of a prayer is determined not by its intensity but **by its origin**. In evaluating prayer we should inquire who is doing the praying--our determined hearts or the Holy Spirit? If the prayer originates with the Holy Spirit, then the wrestling can be beautiful and wonderful; **but if we are the victims of our own overheated desires, our praying can be as carnal as any other act**.

**A.W. Tozer** [114]

---

[113] Sproul, R.C., *Truths We Confess*, P&R Publishing, Phillipsburg, NJ, 2006

[114] Tozer, A.W. - *This World: Playground or Battleground*, Christian Publications, 1989

P51 Mustang (18)

# Supplication (18.6)

"Is anyone among you suffering? Let him pray. Is anyone cheerful? Let him sing praise. Is anyone among you sick? Let him call for the elders of the church, and let them pray over him, anointing him with oil in the name of the Lord. And the prayer of faith will save the one who is sick, and the Lord will raise him up. And if he has committed sins, he will be forgiven. Therefore, confess your sins to one another and pray for one another, that you may be healed. The prayer of a righteous person has great power as it is working"

**James 5:13-17**

**Nehemiah 1:5-11**
What elements of his prayer do you see?

_____

_____

**Isaiah 38:1-8**     Is there anything remarkable about Hezekiah's prayer?

_____

_____

**Daniel 9:1-19**     What is Daniel's attitude in prayer?

_____

_____

"Prayer is spiritual communication between man and God, a two-way relationship in which man should not only talk to God but also listen to Him. Prayer to God is like a child's conversation with his father. It is natural for a child to ask his father for the things he needs."

**Billy Graham**

| Arsenal

## Special Orders (18.7)

It is worth repeating Tozer's words:
**"The spiritual quality of a prayer is determined not by its intensity but by its origin"**

Scripture encourages us to pray without ceasing. Throughout the day, we might pray simple, short prayers based on the momentary circumstances that we encounter. A momentary prayer of thanksgiving or prayer for protection sets the tone of our attitude toward God.

The well-equipped disciple will also set aside a portion of the day where he/she can withdraw to a quiet place to engage in a conversation with the Lord. As a spiritual "discipline", our daily time with the Lord should be intentional and should include reading and meditation on his word.

There is no doubt we will have days when we just don't "feel spiritual". But God's wisdom and power are not dependent on our feelings. Those are the days we should simply "get in the way" of the means of grace. "Ok God – my attitude is bad... let's get started", may not sound biblical. But God knows your heart and a simple verse from Scripture or a thought uttered in prayer are easy tools for an awesome God.

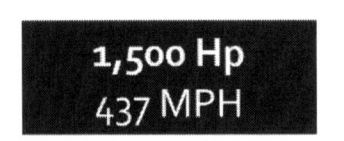

**1,500 Hp**
**437 MPH**

### The power to out run, out dive & out maneuver the best the enemy has to offer

## P51 Mustang (18)

Prayer is not a visit to Santa's lap to list the things we want from God. Prayer is a two-way conversation with the Creator of the Universe in the Holy of Holies. We approach Him with awe and reverence and He speaks to us as we empty our hearts toward him.

**Worship** – Establishes an awesome reverence for our entry into the Holy of Holies. Prayer is not contract negotiation, a debate, or a list of demands. Once we are in His presence, we approach Him with the honor that He is due.

God is unlimited in his sovereign power, and He is infinite in wisdom and perfect in his love. Before you look at your own problems, see Him for who He is.

**Confession** – Confession is not a vain repetition of something we learned to say as a child. Confession is not an incantation or for the sake of penance. Confession should not be "broad-brushed" or watered-down.

David's confession after he committed adultery and murdered Uriah was not "Gee God, if I did anything wrong today, please forgive me". His prayer was specific. "Against you and you alone have I sinned". "Purge me from my iniquities".

If you fell into a septic tank, you would not reach for a tissue. You would run to the shower to get rid of the filth. You did not "misspeak". You lied! You did not "fudge" on your taxes. You cheated! You did not "allow your eyes to wander". You lusted! Real confession can be stark, specific and harsh. Deal with it. Sin is filthy and disgusting in God's eyes. Because of it, He put his Son on a Roman cross.

"The sacrifices of God are a broken and contrite heart". Confession is true biblical sorrow coupled with an awesome reflection on the price that Christ paid. Not "Oh woe is me", but "Oh wow" – because He loves me that much.

Confession is not about condemnation. It's not about a promise to "do better". Confession puts our sins in God's hands and from those hands, He grants his gift of mercy.

| Arsenal

**Thanksgiving** – a true and honest reflection on the many blessings in our life. True thanksgiving is built on "Ebenezer" stones of remembrance, recalling his goodness and provision, and the knowledge that for most (if not all) of those blessings, we did not "deserve" them. Like confession, make thanksgiving specific – recall specifically how God has worked in situations – and continue to add more Ebenezer stones to your collection.

**Supplication** – Reflecting on the needs of others will help you put your own needs in their proper place. When the job is not going well, utter a prayer for a jobless friend. When you can't get over the stomach problems, say a prayer for a friend with cancer. Following up on God's answers to those prayers will lead to encouragement.

**Petition** – There is no such thing as a "small prayer". God calls us to prayer in all circumstances. The lost dog, the lost car keys, etc., as well as the larger things in life – marriage, kids, job, and health. We bring those to the throne of God with a perspective that His plan and His will are much greater than ours so that we can honestly pray "Thy will be done".

> "I have read the lives of many eminent Christians who have been on earth since the Bible days. Some of them, I see, were rich and some poor. Some were learned and some unlearned...some were Calvinists and some were Arminians. Some have loved to use a liturgy and some chose to use none. **But one thing I see they all had in common. They have all been men of prayer**"
>
> **J.C. Ryle** [115]

---

[115] George, Jim, *A Man After God's Own Heart*, Harvest House Publishers 2002, Eugene, Oregon

P51 Mustang (18)

# What's Next?

## Warrior 2

The second study in the Warrior series takes us into the details of the daily battles that define the life of a follower of Christ.

Warrior's continuing theme is built around the words of Thomas Brooks.

> "Beloved in our dearest Lord,
> Christ, the Scripture, your own hearts, and Satan's devices, are the four prime things that should be first and most studied and searched. If any cast off the study of these, they cannot be safe here, nor happy hereafter. It is my work as a Christian, but much more as I am a Watchman, to do my best to discover the fullness of Christ, the emptiness of the creature, and the snares of the great deceiver"

We are called to the Spiritual battlefield. We are called to be aware of Satan's devices. But our enemy is not one, but three, as Satan uses the world (culture), and our own flesh against us on the Spiritual battlefield.

## Warrior 3

The third study in the Warrior series will be focused on trials, suffering and adversity in the Christian life. The Nazi assault on humanity and the Jewish race in what we call the "Holocaust" will play a prominent role in the third installment of the Warrior study.

| Arsenal

# Continued........

Made in the USA
Columbia, SC
29 July 2019